Role of Niche and Disruptive Technologies in India's Deterrence and War Fighting Capabilities

38th USI NATIONAL SECURITY PAPER 2021

Role of Niche and Disruptive Technologies in India's Deterrence and War Fighting Capabilities

Lt Gen PJS Pannu, PVSM, AVSM, VSM (Retd)

United Service Institution of India

New Delhi (India)

Vij Books India Pvt Ltd
New Delhi (India)

Published by

Vij Books India Pvt Ltd
(Publishers, Distributors & Importers)
2/19, Ansari Road
Delhi – 110 002
Phones: 91-11-43596460, 91-11-47340674
Mob: 98110 94883
e-mail: contact@vijpublishing.com
web : www.vijbooks.in

First Published in India in 2021

ISBN: 978-93-90917-44-0

Contents

Introduction

India's security environment has been marked by historical land border disputes with Pakistan and China. Future contests are expected to open into the Indo-Pacific oceans, mainly posed by China. Our favourable geostrategic location comes with challenges—from the neighbouring Af-Pak region, the epicentre of global terrorism[1] on one side and a 'revisionist-expansionist global power' China on the other. Today, the militaries of the three nuclear-armed powers are actively deployed on borders, tagged as the most dangerous place in the world. It is not only the boots on the ground, 'under nuclear overhang' that matters, but it is *the rapidly increasing disruptive military technology differential that is causing a tilt in the balance of power*. Technology is rapidly transforming all military doctrinal discourses, pushing the world into a 'grey zone'. In the last two decades, the new security paradigm has given rise to a Hybrid War where all elements of destruction were thrown in, making it difficult to differentiate between 'war and peace', 'friend or foe' or frontier from the hinterland. In such changing times, Indian Armed Forces have continued to reinvent themselves, facing threats from conventional wars to nuclear deterrence and then facing a Proxy War situation in combination with border skirmishes with 'technological overhang'. *The advent of Covid-19 (Bio-War) has catapulted Chinese belligerence to another level,* resulting in global response such as activation of 'QUAD'; this among deteriorating international cohesion is heating up chances of war where use of technology would be seen as the greatest cause of disruption.[2]

---

1   Lt. General B.S. Pawar, "Threats, Challenges and Vulnerabilities", in *The New Arthashastra: A Security Strategy for India*, ed. Gurmeet Kanwal (India: Harper Collins, 2016), p. 61

2   Please read, International Finance Corporation, "The Impact of COVID-19

Disruptive Technology

Disruptive Technology is the sum of cutting edge and transformative technologies that are leading a change, making current systems based on traditional technologies redundant. This causes a serious dislocation in the traditional way industry, military or a nation runs its business. The Fourth Industrial age (4.0) has brought in 'Information' as a new paradigm where operations have become more complex as threats are difficult to assimilate. Nations have understood the value of Artificial Intelligence (AI), linked to communications and Technology. There would be no place for stand-alone analogous military equipment in high tempo tech-based warfare. The decision making would be complex as Information Operations (IO) would need highly developed Decision Support Systems (DSS) to cut down the OODA (Observe-Orient-Decide-Act) loop. To counter the impact of disruptive technology should be to not only nullify the technological edge of the adversary, but to *build technological deterrence through superiority, making their Military Systems redundant.*

Technological Deterrence is the new security assurance benchmark. In this context, Indian Armed Forces must maintain a high-tech edge for the purpose of discouraging an attack from adversaries with fear of punishment. This edge should dissuade the adversary from military or destructive action through building 'Science and Technology' superiority to act as a deterrence. This would include employment of the physical Force, powered by uncompromising technological capability. *Tech-power should be the main component of Comprehensive National Power (CNP) as it alone provides technological deterrence.*

The Chinese Threat

China is sharply focused on securing regional dominance through building "a networked, precision-strike capability." Beijing seeks modernization in integrated command-and-control, network-

---

on Disruptive Technology Adoption in Emerging Markets", Work Bank Group, 18 February 2021, https://www.ifc.org/wps/wcm/connect/537b9b66-a35c-40cf-bed8-6f618c4f63d8/202009-COVID-19-Impact-Disruptive-Tech-EM.pdf?MOD=AJPERES&CVID=njn5xG9.

centric systems emphasizing joint service approach across the full spectrum of warfare operations. "By 2020, they will have caught up. By 2025, they will be better than us. By 2030, they will dominate the industries."[3] An Air University study states that if Quad systems are not integrated to effectively execute at the speed of 2030 with hypersonic Mach 5 weapons across thousands of miles and with autonomous targeting decisions, then the Quad will not be able to effectively deter. *There is a technological arms race,* and the speed of fielding and integration matters over the next decade. The way to win is to achieve integration first.[4] A comparison is necessary to know where China is likely to stand against any future global response.

Major Weapon Systems Comparison (2030–2040 Estimates)

Weapon Systems	US	Australia	Japan	India	Quad Total	China
5th-generation fighters	1321	72	147	0	**1,468**	**200**
Bombers	88	0	0	0	**88**	**150–172**
Major-surface combatants	78	12	54	22	**166**	**150**
Submarines	25	12	22	24	**83**	**70**
Aircraft carriers	5	0	0	3	**8**	**2**

Note: All US numbers at 50 percent to account for other global activities and US homeland defence.

---

3   Patrick Tucker, "China Will Surpass US in AI Around 2025, Says Google's Eric Schmidt", *Defence One*, 1 November 2017, https://www.defenseone.com/technology/2017/11/google-chief-china-will-surpass-us-ai-around-2025/142214/.

4   Lt. Col Justin L. Diehl, USAF, "Indo-Pacific Deterrence and the Quad in 2030", *Journal of Indo-Pacific Affairs*, Spring 2021, https://media.defense.gov/2021/Mar/07/2002595021/-1/-1/1/18%20DIEHL.PDF.

Threat to India. The threat from Sino-Pak Collusivity has been growing. Pakistan has got easy access to Chinese military hardware and technology. CPEC works as an economic and military corridor making 'Pak a reliable and a slave partner' for helping Chinese to build a military base at Gwadar. The last three decades have seen an enhanced role of Non-State actors shifting the world's attention away from the conventional to sub-conventional and then non-traditional threats, diverting the world's energies towards fighting GWOT (Global War on Terrorism). Today in the hybrid war conditions, threats can emanate from myriad sources to include terrorism, cyber-attack, unconventional attacks using chemical, nuclear or biological weapons, as well as large scale accidents or natural hazards, each having the potential to do grave damage to the country.[5] However, military experts and strategists have been urging the nation to be ready to face a 'two and half front' scenario.[6] China is using combative diplomacy and debt trapping to align the fence-sitters, threatening them of consequences, should they align with the QUAD. Biological Warfare has been reinvented by China. She is heavily invested in disruptive military technologies that directly challenge India. The collusive threat from Pakistan and China of the high tech war is real. The Belt and Road Initiative (BRI) is a strategic step towards making economic and security inroads into most countries in the world. BRI would be making multipurpose digital corridors along with security, trade and commerce elements intrinsic in it.

Other Threats. Heavy investment in 5G technologies in Pakistan and neighbours of India such as Nepal, Bangladesh, Myanmar, Sri Lanka and Pakistan has serious ramifications for India. India continues to import 70 percent of high tech Military hardware.[7]

---

5   Major General Dhruv Katoch, "International Experience: The Defence Policies of Major Powers", in *The New Arthashastra: A Security Strategy for India*, ed. Gurmeet Kanwal (India: Harper Collins, 2016).

6   Shekhar Gupta, "Breaking the two and a half front siege", The Print, 8 July 2017, https://theprint.in/sg-national-interest/breaking-the-two-and-a-half-front-siege/544542/.

7   Col Manoj Mehrotra, "Evolution of Indian Defence and Security Industry in These Recent Years", Diplomatist, 13 April 2020, https://diplomatist. com/2020/04/13/evolution-of-indian-defence-and-security-industry-in-

Though the Government of India is taking initiatives such as 'make in India' and *Atamnirbharta* (Self Reliance), however, *Import of critical components like chips / semiconductors directly or indirectly sourced from China can jeopardise the vision of make in India/ digital India.* India is already facing a Hybrid war situation.[8] This would continue to grow in form, intensity, complexity, means and understanding. Targeting through Artificial Intelligence platforms is fast becoming a reality. There would be a need to guard the hinterland against cyber-attacks by hardening the critical infrastructure in all forms. Deep vertical kinetic attacks in the hinterland cannot be ruled out.

China has caused a major disruption through Covid 19 in 2020-21, effects of which are likely to last a few years. During this time she has attempted to change the global order, manipulate international institutions and create a Counter-QUAD narrative. China has taken all steps to become the sole power ahead of the original plan of achieving this status by 2050. China has shed the policy of external calm and biding time. She is largely invested in Science and Technology (S&T) and graduates more students annually in S&T than the US.[9] China has surged ahead in the Global Innovation Index and stands at 14th position while India ranks 48th.[10] Large dual-use R&D initiatives have been taken, with initial capabilities built on copying and reverse engineering. Combined with R&D and access to rare earth materials, China has been able to significantly enhance her Military and industrial capacity. China has made significant investments in Space, Cyber

---

these-recent-years/.

8   Shilpa Phadnis, "This is How India can Reduce its China Dependence in Electronics", The Times of India, January 7 2021, https://timesofindia.indiatimes.com/business/this-is-how-india-can-reduce-its-china-dependence-in-electronics/articleshow/80135186.cms.

9   Michael T. Nietzel, "U.S. Universities Fall Further Behind China in Production of STEM PhDs", Forbes, 7 August 2021, https://www.forbes.com/sites/michaeltnietzel/2021/08/07/us-universities-fall-behind-china-in-production-of-stem-phds/?sh=687ca6114606.

10 Soumitra Dutta, Bruno Lanvin, and Sacha Wunsch-Vincent, "Global Innovation Index 2020", Cornell SC Johnson College of Business, 2020, https://www.wipo.int/edocs/pubdocs/en/wipo_pub_gii_2020.pdf.

and Rocket technologies and incrementally exported Military hardware to its allies.

Chinese Belligerent Military Action in Eastern Ladakh. The clash on the Northern borders starting with hand to hand, club fighting, saw the quick deployment of forces at multiple points with use of IW and high tech surveillance to capture data and information during border talks. They pulled out from the Moldo sector with speed, getting India to release pressure on the Kailash ranges.[11] *Such action must be seen as the 'test bed' and could work as the data collected from Indian responses.* Such a cycle of operations and data reservoirs is useful to programme the DSS to shorten the OODA loop next time. PLA has created a digital wall of electronic surveillance all along the borders with India, and in combination with satellite surveillance, has *created the condition of intelligentization in warfare.* Chinese disengagement from LAC did not result in demilitarisation, but just the opposite of it, with a large number of rocket units showing up in the depth areas, and reorganisation of PLA formations into integrated Brigade Groups. China has announced recruitment programmes in Tibet and plans to build more infrastructure on the plateau with priority to the border areas. It is rapidly upgrading the airbases, missile sites and logistic support through a large rail-road-tunnel network. PLA reportedly has begun field-testing UAVs in transportation and resupply by conducting exercises using UAVs to air-drop ammunition and medical supplies.[12] PLA has increasingly utilised UAVs to undertake small-scale resupply missions, and it may use UAV technology to boost the tempo of operations along the borders. The PLA's increasing use of UAVs may be an early indicator that it plans to employ UAVs in a wider range of missions.

---

11 Lt. Gen H. S. Panag (Retd), "If India loses grip on Kailash Range, PLA will make sure we never get it back", The Print, 12 November 2020, https://theprint.in/opinion/if-india-loses-grip-on-kailash-range-pla-will-make-sure-we-never-get-it-back/542327/.

12 Eli Tirk and Kieran Green, "Sustaining China's Sovereignty Claims: The PLA's Embrace of Unmanned Logistics", Jamestown Foundation, May 21, 2021, https://jamestown.org/wp-content/uploads/2021/05/Read-the-5-21-21-Issue-in-PDF.pdf?x76120.

The WTC without doubts is building muscle and demonstrating High technological hardware. Parading most of their newly built war machines such as J 20 ac. The anti-aircraft missile and rocket artillery are the fifth and sixth new sets of equipment that entered service with the PLA Xinjiang Military Command plateau forces in May 2020[13]; the missile system and the rocket artillery have been identified as the HQ-17A field air defence missile system and the PHL-11 122 mm calibre self-propelled multiple rocket launcher systems.[14] China's National Day military parade in Beijing in 2019 also paraded the most advanced field air defence missile system - "a single PHL-11 that can carry 40 rockets and provide strong firepower," reported the *Global Times*.[15] Unconfirmed internet reports indicate deployment of DF-21Cs near the Karakoram pass. However, there is confusion on whether these are DF-21Cs or DF-26s. That's because the DF-26s were with the PLA RF's 646 Brigade, Base 64 in 2019 and 2020.[16]

Indian Defence Industrial Complex. Our Defence Industrial Complex needs a close examination in the current challenges that we face. While China is no more cautious of hiding their intentions and has clearly spelt out that the borders would be settled on their terms. Indian Armed Forces once again have made rapid military imports to meet urgent needs to fill up deficiencies mainly borne out of technological deficit. India, as a routine, has been dependent on the import of arms and equipment. The target of 70 percent self-reliance in defence procurement set for 2005 is yet to be achieved. Currently, India's self-reliance is considered to be hovering around 35-40 percent. According to SIPRI (Stockholm International Peace Research Institute) India in 2011-15 was the world's largest importer of major weapons, with a 14 percent global share.

---

13 Liu Xuanzun, "PLA Xinjiang Military Command gets new anti-aircraft missile, rocket artillery", Global Times, May 26, 2021, https://www.globaltimes.cn/page/202105/1224528.shtml.

14 Ibid.

15 Ibid.

16 Suyash Desai, "The PLA Insight: Issue No. 100", Takshila Institution, May 28, 2021, https://mailchi.mp/fc12aaa0ebd0/the-pla-insight-issue-no-100?e=823aa80e84.

And from 2016-20 the second largest with a 9.5 percent global share[17] The OFB (Ordnance Factory Board) with 41 factories, 13 development centres and 9 Institutes of learning, produces legacy military hardware. In addition, there are nine DPSUs (Defence Public Sector undertakings) such as HAL, BEL, BEML, MDL, MDNL, GSL, HSL, BDL and Garden Reach Shipbuilders and Engineers Limited. Both DPSUs and OFs are administered by the Department of Defence Production, MoD. Both sets of Industries have their own research and Development units, although overall R&D activities are met by the DRDO, which has over 50 labs spread all across the country. Despite numerous reform measures undertaken under the ambit of the Make in India programme, the Indian Defence industry suffers from several legacy issues that need to be addressed to establish an efficient and credible defence industrial base.

The national aim for India is to achieve momentous economic development and focused technological progress for the country and its people - in an environment for sustainable human security, discernible stability and substantial prosperity - where individual genius and aspirations can flourish, leading to the collective well-being of the state, while assuming India's rightful place in the emerging regional and global order, i.e. a regional leader by 2030 and a major Global player by 2050.[18] To be able to achieve this objective, India has to take very measured strides to adopt high tech that can cover the gap with immediate neighbours. To aspire to regional leadership, India must focus on matching Chinese capabilities in the next 8-10 years and global standards over 25 years. China is our neighbour and is aspiring to be a superpower by 2050, giving us a direct challenge to revolutionise our growth and military capability.

---

17 Pieter D. Wezemam, Alexandra Kuimova and Siemon T. Wezeman, "Trends in International Arms Transfers, 2020", SIPRI Fact Sheet, March 2021, p. 6, https://sipri.org/sites/default/files/2021-03/fs_2103_at_2020.pdf.

18 Lt. Gen Philip Campose (Retd), *A National Security Strategy for India: A Way Forward* (New Delhi: KW Publishers, 2018), p. 154

India's Current Deterrence. This hinges around maintaining a large conventional force and having a reasonable nuclear weapon capability. This capability is evenly matched by our adversaries. Conventional deterrence can be circumvented by the adversary's strategy and plans. Nuclear weapons induce fear of survival; human behaviour in such circumstances is unreliable for rational thinking and erratic for inducing actions that one expects the adversary to take.[19] There is no dispute that nuclear weapons are not meant for war fighting; therefore, relevance for its deterrence is gradually eroding, especially in Hybrid Warfare conditions. India, Pakistan and China have had nuclear weapons for over three decades, this certainly checkmated the conventional forces, but threats of Proxy Wars or limited wars like Kargil and skirmishes on the LAC continue. The threat dynamics have therefore been worked around grey operations - the Hybrid Wars. Raids by the special forces referred loosely as 'surgical strikes' remain usable to instil fear in the minds of an adversary. As we see the direction that warfare is taking, the *actual deterrence shall come from use of technology* which is highly usable and deniable in the same plane. *Technological deterrence is fast emerging as the alternative to nuclear deterrence.*

Revolution in Military Affairs (RMA). RMA would have to be led by a transformation that makes the Military into fighting high-tech 'autonomous' rather than currently 'analogous' battles. Established the fact that Future Wars are going to be technology-based and technology-driven, *the Digital warfare would draw new baselines for making ICT (Information Communication Technology) a new leader to trigger this change.* With the rapid growth of technology and trade, countries are using technological deterrence for arm twisting for securing business and trade. The Belt and Road Initiative of China makes it possible to club Military and Technological 'Right of Way' to pursue and promote business interests. Therefore, large investments in technology military hardware are going into paddling the doctrine of *'winning wars without fighting'.*

---

19 Lt Gen Prakash Menon, *The Strategy Trap: India and Pakistan under the Nuclear Shadow* (New Delhi: Wisdom Tree, 2019), p. 191

For discussing the disruptive technologies in warfare, applications of military technology are being discussed following Parts:

Part I: Non - Contact and Non- Kinetic applications.

Part II: Non- Kinetic and Kinetic attacks.

Part III: Contact and Non-Kinetic applications.

Part VI: Contact and Kinetic attacks.

Part V: Technology enablers and the future.

Part VI: Emerging warfare concepts and new age technologies.

Part I: Non-Contact and Non-Kinetic Applications

In 2004, the UN Secretary General's High-Level Panel on Threats, Challenges and Change in their report, titled '*A More Secure World: Our shared responsibility*' identified six clusters and challenges: wars between states; violence between states including Civil Wars; large scale human rights abuses and genocide; poverty, infectious diseases and environmental degradation; *nuclear, radiological, chemical and biological weapons*; terrorism and transnational organised crime. *The security threats and challenges went beyond the traditional concept of security.*[1]

The PLA's doctrine of 'three warfares' - that takes recourse to Cyber, electronic and self-sanctified versions of 'legal' warfare is factored into her overall combat power and "Integrated Network Electronic Warfare" (INEW) gives these an ability to persecute these with central control.[2] Certain use cases in technology can deliver Non-Kinetic punches in a manner that that adversary may capitulate even before the first bullet is fired. *Nations would endeavour to achieve their political objective short of an outright war. Offensive use of Information Warfare*, especially in cyberspace, and options of Non-Contact War will give the adversary the ability to cause disruption and destruction and degrade war potential even before the battle is joined.[3] This of course would be laced with strategy

---

1   Arvind Gupta, *How India Manages Its National Security* (New Delhi: Penguin Books, 2018), pp. 267-269.

2   Lt. Gen Gautam Banerjee, *China's Great War Machine in the Sino-Indian Context,* (New Delhi: Wisdom Tree, 2016), pp. 111-112.

3   Lt. General B.S. Pawan, "Threats, Challenges and Vulnerabilities", in *The New Arthashastra: A Security Strategy for India,* ed. Gurmeet Kanwal (India: Harper Collins, 2016), p. 60

and statecraft but damages such attacks can cause are very credible and long lasting. Nations can remain locked into this segment for endless periods without firing a shot. This is somewhat a Cold War scenario, but the *damaging applications of technology* can catapult into Kinetic engagements. While there are numerous 'non-contact disruptive technologies' with relevant use cases, the most significant ones in this segment are discussed in the succeeding paragraphs.

Cyber Warfare. This way of war is universally acknowledged to be leading the twenty-first century war, which would certainly be 'cyber centric' if not fully led by the cyber theatre. Cyberspace has been accepted as the fifth domain of war that nations need to protect and exploit for offensive operations. The militarisation of cyberspace and development of cyber weapons are raising the spectre of a cyber war.[4] In fact, Cyber-attacks are soon emerging as the hidden mother of all Wars. The digitisation of Warfare with applications that connect the human mind to war machines puts the cyber ecosystem at the core of all functions. Cyber Warfare would mean hitting the electronic or digital nerve of the adversary while securing your own. It covers a very large canvas from Information Systems to data that moves the digital platforms which are networked. The Cyber domain can be compared with the human body that connects and combines all the vital organs in particular, a combination of 'Brain and Heart'. Brain is the nerve centre and the heart is the prime mover of data as power. Any of these get hit, the system shall paralyse. Since cyber networks comprise, the number of computers interlinked and fused together through the network, if any computer in the network gets compromised, acts as the weakest link that compromises the entire network. The Networks and Data containing Information would remain constant targets of the adversary. *There are no defined Cyber borders – it is all pervasive.* All critical infrastructure such as Power supply, movement means such as railways, aircrafts and military platforms can be attacked. One wonders if there would be more

---

4   Lt. Gen Davinder Kumar, "Cyber Security: Status and Imperatives", *The New Arthashastra: A Security Strategy for India*, ed. Gurmeet Kanwal (India: Harper Collins, 2016), p. 273

alarm if "major pipeline" was to be shut down by a cyberattack," another way of enforcing oil embargo.

Electric Power Grids are regulated and controlled through a network of computers. A knock on the power cyber grid shall bring the country to a grinding halt. Worse is, as the government is rapidly moving to e-governance, ending the need of maintaining physical files, an attack would not only make these files and data inaccessible to us but also can steal the files. A case in point is an attack on the website of CDA that contains data of all Defence officers. Similar attacks can paralyse Airlines, Banking, Defence, Health services, logistics-supply chain, e- market, e-governance etc, and trigger a man-made disaster. Even though, firewalls, encryptions and protocols are regularly updated, what is most concerning is that, most often, it is the staff of the enterprise managing the database- developers, administrators, and others, who end up creating an unsecured environment facilitating a cyber-attack.[5]

In recent years, attacks targeting critical infrastructure and businesses have surged. These include the 2017 WannaCry and Not Petya ransomware attacks, the 2015 attack on Ukrainian power grids and 2010 Stuxnet attack on Iranian nuclear reactors.[6] Those systems that are high security networks are classified as critical infrastructures and are given top priority in Cyber Security. In India, National Critical Information Infrastructure protection Centre (NCIIPC) is mandated under Article 70 A (2008), to look at the designated critical information infrastructure (CIIs) and evolve, policies and procedures to protect them from Cyber Attacks.[7] However, with imported chipsets or computer hardware and

---

5   Vinit Goenka (eds), *Data Sovereignty: The Pursuit of Supremacy,* (New Delhi: Penman Books, 2019), p. 87

6   Lt. Gen Davinder Kumar, "Cyber Security: Status and Imperatives", *The New Arthashastra: A Security Strategy for India,* ed. Gurmeet Kanwal (India: Harper Collins, 2016), p. 279

7   Sameer Patil, "Cyber-attacks on critical infrastructure: Is India ready?", Hindustan Times, 20 May 2021, https://www.hindustantimes.com/opinion/cyber-attacks-on-critical-infrastructure-is-india-ready-101621514744151.html.

software, it is not the most assured way of securing these networks. The blockchain technology and Quantum Computing is the need of the hour for securing and encrypting the networks of critical infrastructure. The solution lies in designing (IITs are competent) and fabricating semiconductors. Till the time our domestic industry can achieve fabrication standards, we must build sufficient labs to test the foreign supply chain to weed out infected or substandard Chipsets and semiconductors. Similarly, we cannot rely on 5G rollout from suspect international companies, which would run IOT programmes. Any compromise on this is risking handing over our Command and Control in the hands of an adversary. For Military platforms, it would be essential to build military grade secrecy and protection from interference. The basic 'attack identity' is the IP address, it is essential that Military equipment as also critical infrastructure must create 'Non IP' systems, without addresses that are known or recognised by other agencies. DARPA has been working on IP address less connections. The Distributed Denial of Service (DDOS) are becoming more severe; their speed has increased to over 300 gigabits per second. The amount of data coming at this speed can easily overwhelm most servers and cause networks to crash.[8] Cyber Espionage, cyber terrorism and social media amalgam adds to the vulnerability of individuals and who may not be able to get any institutional support due to either lack or very nascent legal provisions. Electronic Warfare would remain a prime focus in the future battlefield as cyber- electro-magnetic spectrum would make heavy electronic emissions on the battlefield. Hiding electronic signatures would be difficult yet important. Increasing shift of electronics emissions into tubes such as Optical fibre would become inescapable and shall *conjoin the underground battlefield concept*. Electronic emission suppressors and reflectors would be mandatory for survival.[9]

---

8   Arvind Gupta, *How India Manages Its National Security* (New Delhi: Penguin Books, 2018), pp. 313.

9   "Synergy: New Age Technologies and Military – Indian Context", Journal of the Centre for Joint Warfare Studies, February 2021, https://cenjows.in/upload_images/pdf/Synergy-Journal-Feb-2021-Release-on-22-Feb-2021.pdf

Information and Psychological War. This is leading the modern warfare pack. Effective psywar is the ability to put forward and defend an idea, or to offer a better way that is appealing to the recipient and not merely the giver.[10] Intelligence agencies use soft power as an influence tool. Dislocating the mind of an adversary and capturing it would mean hitting the centre of gravity without a physical attack. The 'chaos theory' is the most organised way of fighting this war. A Chaotic mind is a defeated mind. Reactions can be mapped by different individuals and groups after applying a shock. This 'reaction repository' is data that can design the next wave of chaos. The reactions to each narrative are mapped and modified. This form of warfare exploits the existing fault lines in the nation and creates events to accentuate these. Fault lines also erupt based on the different value systems in the nation which define the character of the nation. In democratic countries it becomes extremely difficult to cover the vulnerability shown by these differences making data collection and writing of narratives relatively easy. Today, AI applications are aggregating this data and using it to manipulate the minds. Once that is done, the targeted adversary would defeat itself when there is a calibrated application of shock. It is easy to build narratives and counter narratives if the data of the adversary is available. Information warfare is a combination of cyber, space, electronic, propaganda, psychological, media and social media wars.[11] Information Warfare targets the minds of different segments of people. Starting from young minds attending schools or playing computer games to higher age groups. For each group, it would be difficult to differentiate between truth and lies. Each theme exploits the vulnerability of people in different sections and throws thematic scares to target human psychology. Increase in mass shooting in night clubs, educational institutions and religious places has been achieved by radicalization of vulnerable minds on the internet,

---

10 Vikram Sood, "The Future of Intelligence", *The New Arthashastra: A Security Strategy for India*, ed. Gurmeet Kanwal (India: Harper Collins, 2016), p. 124

11 Lt. Gen Philip Campose (Retd), *A National Security Strategy for India: A Way Forward* (New Delhi: KW Publishers, 2018), p. 33

which has become a potent tool of warfare. Recruitment drives for ISIS and other radical groups and use of the dark web for supply and arms and ammunition has already been in vogue.

Space Warfare. This is now seen as an essential and most significant domain of modern warfare. Military profession teaches us the importance of 'high ground' and 'information' as its key factors of success. Space is the 'ultimate high ground' that makes it possible for an ordinary citizen to watch the world from God's eye, even views of the battlefield. Space Wars would be relevant because of the universal application of space technology to most digital platforms. PNT (Place Navigation and Time), Communication, Surveillance, planetary dominance and counterspace assets would dominate the future security paradigm. Increasingly 5G and beyond - IoT (Internet of Thing) would be all pervasive in moving IoMT (Internet of Military Things) for strategic applications in warfighting. Surveillance and Target Acquisition would be passed over to Satellites that provide better resolution, clearly identify targets and engage with precision missile munitions.

There are rapid technology upgrades taking place in the space domain and catching up would not be easy unless early steps are taken. China has invested in QC-QT (Quantum Computing and Technology), which would harden most of their satellites. China is the only country to land its spacecraft (Chang'-4) on the far side of the moon, with rover sending data from and operating in temperatures below -300 degrees Fahrenheit.[12] China would now have access to rare materials from the moon.[13] China has also successfully landed a spacecraft on Mars in May 2021 in the planet's northern hemisphere. Only the Americans have really

---

12 "China's Chang'e-4 lunar rover lands on moon's far side, sends back images", The Hindu, 3 January 2019, https://www.thehindu.com/sci-tech/science/ chinas-change-4-lunar-rover-lands-on-moons-far-side-sends-back-images/ article25899235.ece.

13 Deng Xiaoci, "Zhuong sends back signals, marking success of Tianwen-I's landing on Mars", Global Times, 15 May 2021, https://www.globaltimes.cn/ page/202105/1223518.shtml.

mastered landing on Mars until now. All other countries that have tried have either crashed or lost contact soon after reaching the surface.[14]

Having put three manned space labs in the Low Orbit, it is rapidly developing both ISR and PNT satellites.[15] Their Beidou satellite gives her independence from the GPS.[16] China plans to establish a global 24-hour, all-weather earth remote sensing system and a global satellite navigation system.[17] The Chinese company is dedicated to creating and operating a 13,000-satellite broadband constellation.[18] The plans consist of sub-constellations ranging from 500 - 1,145 kilometres. To this China has added **"satellite internet"** to a list of "new infrastructures". Given the belligerence of China against India, their space edge poses a challenge to the world, and Indian Space assets in case of a military confrontation. With assistance from China, Pakistan is investing incrementally in its Space and Upper Atmosphere Research Organisation (SUPARCO) with the budgetary allocation of approx. $34 million to include Multi-Mission Satellite (PaKSat-MM1).[19]

---

14 Katerina Ang, "China becomes second country to drive a rover on Mars", The Washington Post, 22 May 2021, https://www.washingtonpost.com/world/2021/05/22/china-successfully-deploys-rover-explore-mars/.

15 Jonathan Amos, "China space station: Shenzhou-12 delivers first crew to Tianhe module", BBC, 17 June 2021, https://www.bbc.com/news/science-environment-57504052.

16 "China will complete its Beidou Navigation Satellite Network, gaining independence from US-owned GPS", Firstpost, 15 June 2020, https://www.firstpost.com/tech/science/china-will-complete-its-beidou-navigation-satellite-network-gaining-independence-from-us-owned-gps-8484011.html.

17 Meng Qingsheng, "Gaofen satellites upgrade China's civilian mapping practice", CGTN, 15 December 2019, https://news.cgtn.com/news/2019-12-15/Gaofen-satellites-upgrade-China-s-civilian-mapping-practice-Mrt66LeUUg/index.html.

18 Andrew Jones, "China is developing plans for a 13,000-satellite megaconstellation", Space News, 21 April 2021, https://spacenews.com/china-is-developing-plans-for-a-13000-satellite-communications-megaconstellation/.

19 "Pakistan set to launch space programme to keep an eye on Indian side: Report", The Economic Times, 29 April 2018, https://economictimes.indiatimes.com/news/science/pakistan-set-to-launch-space-programme-to-

The US military spends $35 billion each year on space, which is twice NASA's budget. The US military relies heavily on their private sector to deliver space solutions.[20] SpaceX is planning to launch a global constellation of 4,425 satellites which will provide a total throughput of 23.70 Terabytes per second — a capability which will be leveraged by the US military. The rapid miniaturisation and cost reduction of the civil space sector in the US has been picked up by the US military. Project Blackjack under DARPA, for instance, envisages the use of multiple constellations launched and operated by the private sector to provide a resilient, persistent and reliable data network for troops and equipment on the ground.[21]

India became the seventh country to launch its own satellite using the SLV-3 rocket in July 1980. Currently, India has two operational orbital Launch vehicles, with the Polar Satellite Launch Vehicle (PSLV) and the Geosynchronous Satellite Launch Vehicle (GSLV). With these two vehicles, India conducted seven launches in 2018, just a fraction of over 60 total launches.[22] The PSLV has launched over 46 successful missions. It has also launched around 300 satellites of more than 30 countries. In February 2017, ISRO (PSLV-C37) launched 104 satellites belonging to different countries in a single rocket, which is a record.[23] India has recently

---

keep-an-eye-on-indian-side-report/articleshow/63960215.cms.

20 C. Todd Lopez, "U.S. Space Effort's Future Hinges on Private Industry", US Dept of Defense, 28 July 2020, https://www.defense.gov/Explore/News/Article/Article/2291577/us-space-efforts-future-hinges-on-private-industry/.

21 "DARPA deploys two Mandrake 2 satellites under Blackjack project", Airforce Technology", 8 July 2021, https://www.airforce-technology.com/news/darpa-two-mandrake-2-satellites-blackjack-project/.

22 T E Narasimhan, "Year in space: Isro gears up for busy 2019 after successful 2018", Business Standard, 24 December 2018, https://www.business-standard.com/article/economy-policy/year-in-space-isro-gears-up-for-busy-2019-after-successful-2018-118122400006_1.html.

23 "PSLV-C37 Successfully Launches 104 Satellites in a Single Flight", ISRO, 15 February 2017, https://www.isro.gov.in/pslv-c37-succesfully-launches-104-satellites-single-flight#:~:text=In%20its%20thirty%20ninth%20flight,Dhawan%20Space%20Centre%20SHAR%2C%20Sriharikota.

raised a Defence Space Agency under HQ Integrated Defence Staff.[24] DRDO is actively engaged in supporting the sector through a dedicated Space Project. India needs to invest in hardening the satellite technology to match the challenges posed by Quantum technologies. ISRO needs to focus on closing this gap with private players as technology partners. Space threat detection, miniaturisation of assets and counter-space kinetic and non-kinetic assets are significant steps to keep Indian space secure. India demonstrated kinetic anti-satellite capability in 2019 named Project Shakti. Increasingly, cyberspace and digital platforms are becoming space dependent and controlled. We are headed to C5 I2 STAR cluster that brings Command, Control, Communication, Computer and Cyber in a single domain, as also brings Target Acquisition as part of the same cluster as the ISR.

ISR (Intelligence Surveillance and Reconnaissance). This pries on the enemy round the clock. 'Knowing the adversary' has always been the most significant part of warfare, with technology becoming its prime-driver, ISR is emerging as a tool to fight precise battles. If an adversary is seen, identified and tracked, it can be targeted, using weapons of choice. Space has emerged as the most important tool for ISR. Most satellites in LEO and MEO are ideal, however, being on the lower orbit, these satellites are mobile and need many satellites requiring a number of passes for constant imagery updates. For military grade imagery, a resolution of less than a meter (sub-metric) is necessary. As technology is improving, it is getting possible to identify the target with a higher spatial resolution. Currently, 25 cm resolution is the best publicly available. The satellite with the highest resolution was probably the KH-8 Gambit, known for imagery better than four inches ground-resolved distance. This resolution may have been enough to see a golf ball, but not read newspapers. A five cm resolution is known to have been developed for spy satellites. American Hubble Space telescope, meant for astronomical research, is likely to be more

---

24 Satish Dua, "HQ Integrated Defence Staff in the National Security Structure", Journal of Defence Studies, Vol. 13, No. 13 (July-September 2019), pp. 53-69, https://idsa.in/system/files/jds/13-3-2019-integrated-defence-staff-in-national-security.pdf.

sensitive than a spy satellite, because the nebulas it is designed to see are too dim to see otherwise, while Earth is bright. They probably have similar optics, but Hubble is forced at infinity focus for universe observation, while a spy satellite might adjust slightly. China is reportedly developing a new telescope with a 300-times larger field of view than the Hubble Space telescope.[25] China is also constantly upgrading China's High Resolution Earth Observation System (CHEOS).

Aerial Photography. Aerial photography through drone cameras is reliable but have a limit to the range they can fly. During Exercise IndspaceX held in Delhi, certain technologies were discussed that make it possible to fly drones in tandem with satellites to beat the weather/cloud cover and /or amplify the pictures of satellites by terrain correlation. The swarm of surveillance drones can be made to fly the same swath of territory being covered real time by the satellite. *Low flying drones, captive to satellite* can bring excellent real time results.   Indian Army currently uses Israeli Heron I for surveillance with a ceiling altitude of 35000 ft and now are set to acquire Heron II with 45 hours endurance.[26] The Navy is using MQ 9B Sea Guardian Drones, a variant of an iconic armed predator. The MQ-9B drone can fly for about 48 hours and carry a payload of about 1,700 kilograms. It will give the Indian Navy the ability to better monitor foreign warships in the southern Indian Ocean, and equip the army to engage targets along the LC or LAC. Airborne Early Warning Aircraft have better ability to detect and recognise targets as compared to surface-based radars, observation systems and ground sensors. The PLA has built the digital surveillance wall along the borders with India for EW and targeting.[27] *The concept*

25 Andrew Jones, "China wants to launch its own Hubble-class telescope as part of space station", Space.com, 20 April 2021, https://www.space.com/china-hubble-class-telescope-for-space-station.

26 "India set to get four Heron long-endurance drones from Israel", The Economic Times, 27 May 2021, https://economictimes.indiatimes.com/news/defence/india-to-shortly-deploy-new-israeli-heron-drones-in-ladakh-lac-sector/articleshow/82973127.cms?from=mdr.

27 "PLA enhancing intelligence, surveillance of border troops amid China-India tensions: Report", ANI News, 8 March 2021, https://www.aninews.in/news/world/asia/pla-enhancing-intelligence-surveillance-of-border-troops-amid-

of unmanned smart borders should be able to carry out unmanned tactical and operational recce. Cyber surveillance, detection and analysis is the emerging field for accessing military intelligence at all levels. AI applications must be used to quickly process the data collected from all the above intelligence feeds and make it available as Common Operating Picture (COP) for decision making at each level.

The PLAAF's inventory of roughly 20 AWACS and airborne early warning and control (AEW&C) aircraft outnumbers the IAF fleet of five aircraft and can change the result of a conflict or a full-fledged war. The KJ -2000 Mainring (based on Ilyushin Il-76), KJ-200 Moth (Shaanxi Y-8), and KJ-500 (Shaanxi Y-9) are China's force multipliers amplifying the capabilities to detect, track, and target threats. The IAF currently operates indigenously developed DRDO AEW&C system, which is based on the Embraer ERJ 145 aircraft, and the EL/W-2090 Phalcon AEW&C installed on the Beriev A-50 platform.

For Special Forces, the information regarding the target areas is readily available for planning strategic level operations. *Special forces can use Nano drones* (18 gms) with a range of 1.5 km, and three thermal cameras. These are robust, single hand control with 25 mins endurance, flying at 8-12 meters per second for intimate and real time reconnaissance of target before strike or make post damage assessments. Such drones are so small that they would hardly get noticed.

Weather and Climate War. This type of war closely follows Sun Tzu's dictum of 'winning without fighting', where an adversary can attempt to exploit the fragile weather and terrain. Weather manipulation is a form of Warfare that is clearly disruptive.[28] This is entirely possible in the younger and unstable Himalayan ranges.

---

china-india-tensions-report20210308234315/.

28 "China has built up its muscle on how to turn weather into a weapon. Can India match up to it?", The Economic Times, 29 October 2019, https:// economictimes.indiatimes.com/prime/economy-and-policy/china-has-built-up-its-muscle-on-how-to-turn-weather-into-a-weapon-can-india-match-up-to-it/primearticleshow/71798844.cms?from=mdr.

Water diversion and control can give a handle to China to create water deficiency or trigger floods at will. There has been historical evidence of seeding clouds by the US in the Vietnam war called Op POPEYE. The US has carried out a considerable amount of research to *weaponize weather*, especially under the Office of Strategic Services, now CIA.[29] Geneva conventions 1978 prohibits military or any other hostile use of environmental technology. Charging clouds or *seeding clouds* can be used to blind the pilots in the valleys by creating dense fog and rain. Creating a *cloud cover over the military concentration* areas to blind the satellites is being tested. Similarly, temperature and atmospheric pressure manipulations can cause cyclones. An explosion in and around the unstable rock plates can *trigger earthquakes or Tsunami*, though there is no evidence of any success of such triggers.

Triggered Nature Attacks. These can be resorted to by the adversary to degrade human ability to fight. *Such indirect attacks are deniable and covered under the act of nature or 'Acts of God'.* The conventional CBRN direct attacks would not be acceptable by the international community as all are banned under the UN conventions.[30] However, these capabilities could be used with changed formulations to be covered under Nature attacks to escape accountability to such protocols by any signatory or member states. Coronavirus attacks should be seen under this category.[31] This would complicate matters, should the imported vaccines be viewed with suspicion, and seen as impacting the reproduction of

---

29 Seymour M. Hersh, "Rainmaking is Used as Weapon by U.S.", The New York Times, 3 July 1972, https://www.nytimes.com/1972/07/03/archives/rainmaking-is-used-as-weapon-by-us-cloudseeding-in-indochina-is.html.

30 Please see, "The International Legal Framework against Chemical, Biological. Radiological and Nuclear Terrorism, United Nations Office on Drugs and Crime, 2016, https://www.unodc.org/documents/terrorism/for%20web%20stories/1-WS%20CBRN%206%20modules/CBRN_module_-_E.pdf.

31 Dr. Nalin Kumar, "View: COVID-19, China's bioweapon warfare strategy and global security", The Economic Times, 8 June 2021, https://economictimes.indiatimes.com/news/defence/view-covid-19-chinas-bioweapon-warfare-strategy-and-global-security/articleshow/83321527.cms?from=mdr.

people of certain DNA, breed or a race. Even news of this kind could create havoc. It is getting difficult to draw lines between fake news or fake products.

Biological War. This war can neither be brushed away and discarded as conspiracy theory, nor dismissed on the pretext that Bio War Conventions do not permit use of Bio weapons. In fact, this is the most usable and deniable weapon that exists in the shades of grey, the band in which Hybrid wars are prosecuted. There are clear pointers that Covid 19 has been the creation of Wuhan labs.[32] This shall remain a matter of dispute since China is neither going to permit inspection / collection of evidence nor being P5, would allow the UN to take cognisance of it. The location of the wet market in Wuhan has only given a good cover for denial. In any case, co-location of the wet market works towards the convenience of extracting viruses from the animals. Covid 19 therefore is a biological weapon for certain. It has destroyed the world and given undue advantage to the aggressor China. Using the covid as the barrage, China has attacked the world militarily. Though Wuhan labs have recently become infamous due to covid, however, many countries have virology labs all over the world. Unit 731 of Japan, was co-located next to the PsOW camp in Manchuria and is known to have been conducting Biological experiments from 1936 onwards, killing thousands of PsOW on experiments by injecting them with Cholera, anthrax, plague, typhoid, syphilis, bubonic plague and parasites.[33] The US has maintained a Biological Weapons Command, establishing labs and running experiments in many parts of the world.[34] Though Geneva Conventions of 1972 prohibits use of bio weapons, in 2001 the US declined to sign the protocols for inspections. It is also widely believed that the Chinese

---

32 "There are clear pointers that Covid 19 has been the creation of Wuhan labs.", *Livemint*, 20 May 2021, https://www.livemint.com/science/health/coronavirus-could-have-been-created-in-wuhan-lab-escaped-from-there-report-11621497728628.html.

33 Justin McCurry, "Japan's sins of the past", The Guardian, 28 October 2004, https://www.theguardian.com/world/2004/oct/28/worlddispatch.justinmccurry.

34 Ibid.

scientists have been working towards weaponizing Covid for the last five years. The spread of H1N1, SARS and the Ebola virus in recent times have caused scares around the world. The new viruses which are born due to changes in Climate and the destruction of habitat can spread from animals to humans. The ability of our public health systems to deal with pandemics is still limited.[35]

Two characteristics make bioweapons an ideal choice for an aggressor — their invisibility and their delayed effect. They can infect the target population, escape undetected, and leave a panicked population and an administration, which is paralysed, in their wake. Sickness and death are not the goal, but fear and uncertainty aimed to breakdown state authority. A good example is the so-called 'anthrax letters' after the September 2001 attack, which created a huge psychological impact despite infecting very few people.[36] Other choices for bioweapons are; anthrax - because it can be released quietly; smallpox - frozen stocks of which are still maintained by the US; tularaemia - known as rabbit fever; and botulism - which is caused by exposure to toxins made by C. botulinum. These are the most toxic substances known to humankind. It attacks the nerves and can lead to respiratory failure. Now, even coronavirus could find itself in the armoury of some nation or terrorist group.

The USSR has had intensive Bio Warfare facilities at par with nuclear weapons. A vector Lab in Siberia was suspected to produce 'smallpox' as a weapon.[37] Similarly, there was a known Anthrax weapons production facility, at Stepnogorsk, Kazakhstan with the capability to produce an estimated 300 metric tons of weaponized

---

35 Arvind Gupta, *How India Manages Its National Security* (New Delhi: Penguin Books, 2018), pp. 268

36 "Amerithrax Investigation Summary", Department of Justice, Government of the U.S., https://www.justice.gov/archive/amerithrax/docs/amx-investigative-summary2.pdf.

37 Filippa Lentzos, "What happened after an explosion at a Russian disease research lab called VECTOR?", *The Bulletin*, 27 November 2019, https://thebulletin.org/2019/11/what-happened-after-an-explosion-at-a-russian-disease-research-lab-called-vector/.

anthrax in eight months.[38] Caroli such programs seem to be very advanced and they don't talk about it.[39] Imagine a Biological weapon in the hands of a terrorist, or a microbiologist becoming a terrorist ? or even worse, terrorists recruit scientists to deploy anthrax.

The 'Convention on the Prohibition of the Development, Production and Stockpiling of Bacteriological (Biological) and Toxin Weapons and on their Destruction', was signed by 103 countries in 1972.[40] It prohibits the development, production, and stockpiling of pathogens or toxins in "quantities that have no justification for prophylactic, protective or other peaceful purposes." Unfortunately, this treaty does not provide for inspections and coercive measures to prevent armament and adherence to protocol. *Bio-warfare is no longer in the realms of fiction. It must be recognised and incorporated into every country's defence protocols.* To face the threat with calmness, the medical fraternity and the public must be educated in epidemiology and control measures. The COVID-19 pandemic has been the closest thing to a mass bio-attack and it is clear that even advanced western nations are far from ready to handle it.

---

38 Andrew C. Weber, Christine L. Parthemore, "Lessons from Kazakhstan: 25 Years of Counting Weapons of Mass Destruction Threats", Belfer Center, Harvard Kennedy School, January 2017, https://www.belfercenter.org/publication/lessons-kazakhstan.

39 Caroline Mortimer, "North Korea could be mass producing biological weapons to unleash smallpox and plague, report warns", Independent, 24 October 2017, https://www.independent.co.uk/news/world/asia/north-korea-biological-weapons-belfer-centre-pyongyang-nuclear-kim-jong-un-smallpox-plague-nerve-gas-korean-war-a8015931.html.

40 "Convention on the Prohibition of the Development, Production and Stockpiling of Bacteriological (Biological) and Toxin Weapons and on their Destruction", United Nations Audiovisual Library of International Law, 10 April 1972, https://legal.un.org/avl/pdf/ha/cpdpsbbtwd/cpdpsbbtwd_e.pdf.

Part II: Non-Contact: Kinetic

As a thumb rule, adversaries do not shoot at each other during the cold war, more so, when the ever-increasing role of technology in warfare makes it possible to use plethora of benign, non-kinetic means of warfare. Should the external situation go out of hand where two sides cannot resolve or avoid a hot conflict, Kinetic application of force may become the only choice, as seen recently (May '21) IDF responding to Hamas's rockets with the Iron dome shield. Similarly, during Operation Desert storm in 1993, saw the US using Patriot missiles in combination with airpower in response to the Scuds of Iraqi forces.[1] *Once the long-distance artillery, air power, rockets or missiles open up, this can be taken as the second stage, where the adversary could be shaping the battle or even using punitive deterrence to stop escalation into a contact battle.* During this stage, certain critical logistic and military infrastructure may be targeted with a view to breaking the will of the adversary and/ or cause serious damage to the military capability of the adversary. This is the next step of the escalation ladder, but without resorting to contact battle. *Belligerent side would still aim to win the battle without fighting a contact war.* In the future wars, stand-off engagements would be more pronounced, making eye-ball to eye-ball contact virtually redundant. Kinetic capabilities would increasingly be sharpened with higher lethality, high precision and longer strike ranges. The target engagement for a stand-off kinetic attack would need better ISR. Target acquisition would need accurate and real time geo-referencing, keep the target locked in

---

1   Major Bryon E. Greenwald, "The History, Development, and Military Significance of Ballistic Missiles on Tactical Operations", School of Advanced Military Studies, United States Army Command and General Staff College Fort Leavenworth, Kansas, 1994, https://apps.dtic.mil/sti/pdfs/ADA293648. pdf.

till sensor-shooter synchronisation delivers a precision attack. The sensors must have the ability to call off the strike before launch, in case target priorities change. This is possible only through spatial - digital and networked platforms. Similarly, counter to such stand-off attacks by the adversary is in having credible Missile Defence, that would need attacks to be intercepted and destroyed before they are delivered. It would be necessary to detect the launch sites of adversaries ahead of time. Passive defensive means certainly include *'hiding and hardening'* own assets.

Strategic Forces. Such forces are usually referred to a club of weapons under one umbrella organisation that controls strategic weapons. The weapons and resources used are likely to be strategic in nature, as such the Strategic Forces at the national level would control these assets. Strategic Forces would in fact control both Non-Kinetic and Kinetic applications for warfare. Satellites can form the offensive arm and also provide platforms from Surveillance and Communications to provide command and control of strategic assets. Chinese in 2015 raised the Strategic Support Force (SFF) to manage the military's space, cyber, and electronic warfare missions.[2] Strategists in PLA regard that "the ability to use space-based systems and deny them to adversaries as central to enabling modern warfare under the conditions of Informatisation".[3] PLA Rocket Force which manages the nuclear arsenal, has also a jurisdiction over the Anti-Satellite (ASAT) capabilities.

Rocket Forces. These are seen as the delivery vehicles for long and medium range delivery of payloads. The ever-increasing ranges, enhanced accuracy and lethality of conventional warheads make rocket forces the most potent force. It is estimated that 104 Chinese

---

2   John Costello and Joe McReynolds, "China's Strategic Support Force: A Force for a New Era", NDU Press, 2 October 2018, https://ndupress.ndu.edu/Media/News/Article/1651760/chinas-strategic-support-force-a-force-for-a-new-era/.

3   "The race for space: Rising concerns", Daily Hunt, 18 July 2021, https://m.dailyhunt.in/news/india/english/the+daily+guardian-epaper-thdygre/the+race+for+space+rising+concerns-newsid-n199486556.

missiles could strike all or parts of India.[4] These include about a dozen DF-31A (11,000 Kms) and six to twelve DF-31(7,000 kms) missiles capable of reaching all Indian mainland targets. Another dozen DF-21s (2150 kms) have important military targets and towns in range. The remaining missiles can target sections of India's northeast and east coast. As China deploys more road-mobile missiles in future, it will be easier for it to move missiles from the interior to new survivable positions within India' range.[5] China is developing hypersonic rockets where the speed of rockets or missiles is essential for breaking through AD cover or Missile Defence. Hypersonic missiles are manoeuvrable and travel at speeds 5 to 20 times the speed of sound. Emerging threats from North Korea, Iran, and other actors necessitate the establishment of collaborative technologies of space-based sensors and kill capabilities. Pakistan has developed nuclear weapons and integrated them with ballistic missile systems. Its longest-range missile Shaheen 3, could potentially deliver a nuclear-capable warhead into LEO. Both North Korea and Pakistan are assessed to be leaning heavily on the space capability of China and the triad can bring in collusive capability against the world.[6] The U.S. military has been collaborating and learning from Israel's armed forces for decades. Israel's grasp of advanced technologies has made it a valuable partner in developing and deploying missile defence systems. The two countries continue to collaborate on short-range missiles and rocket defence systems. The U.S. Army recently purchased a pair of Iron Dome batteries as an interim option and is considering their long-term viability, demonstrating the importance of Israeli technology in this field.[7] In the meantime,

---

4   Frank O'Donnell and Alexander K. Bollfrass, "The Strategic Postures of China and India: A Visual Guide", Belfer Center, Harvard Kennedy School, March 2020, https://www.belfercenter.org/publication/strategic-postures-china-and-india-visual-guide.

5   Maj Gen PK Mallick, "China's Nuclear and Missile Capabilities: An Overview", Vivekananda International Foundation, VIF Paper, April 2021, https://www.vifindia.org/sites/default/files/China-s-Nuclear-and-Missile-Capabilities-An-Overview.pdf.

6   "The race for space: Rising concerns", Daily Hunt, no. 62

7   Michael Eisenstadt, Henry "Trey" Obering III, Samantha Ravich and

the bilateral missile defence partnership is likely to develop into next-generation capabilities that focus on exploiting new environments such as space.

Weapons of Mass Destruction (WsMD). WsMD are currently clubbed as CBRN (Chemical, Biological, Radiological and Nuclear) weapons. Out of these four domains, Nuclear Weapons are the only ones which have been overtly used, formalised and recognised by the global community, with nations declaring their policies and doctrines. The large-scale devastation that it causes has brought in CTBT and MCTR regimes to limit use weapons and its delivery systems to ensure that more nations do not acquire such capabilities. Till the time NSG did not accommodate India following the agreement with the US, India was not acknowledged as a Nuclear Power. Nuclear weapons are considered as weapons of deterrence rather than war fighting. Countries use doctrines and policies as the instrument to deter, by having declared ambiguous policies used for sabre-rattling and blackmailing.

In Spite of Chemical, Biological and Radiological (CBR) weapons being banned by the Geneva conventions, nations still possess them. These are a preferred choice of nations who do not have Nuclear material and technology. Such weapons are also considered as poor-man's WsMD. Due to the treaties banning the CBR, most nations have not invested in defence against these weapons. Chemical and Radiological weapons have also been covered in this Part as these may be combined with the Kinetic attacks, while Biological weapons have been covered in Part I (Non-Kinetic category). With miniaturization and proliferation of technology, it is possible to orchestrate combined attacks of CBRN weapons in this century of complex nexus that exist between state and non-state actors.

David Pollock, "An Expanded Agenda for U.S.-Israel Partnership: New Technologies, New Opportunities", The Washington Institute for Near East Policy, Policy Watch 3484, 7 May 2021, https://www.washingtoninstitute.org/policy-analysis/expanded-agenda-us-israel-partnership-new-technologies-new-opportunities.

Nuclear Forces. These forces are the military units meant to deploy and operate nuclear weapons usually controlled by the highest national command authority. Today, nine countries are considered as nuclear weapon states. The nuclear balance of power is achieved between these countries through nuclear deterrence, having second or third strike capabilities and/or by diversifying modes of delivery. There is a constant race in not only building nuclear arsenals but also developing technologies around miniaturization, multiple warheads / multiple targets and enhanced lethality while enjoying nuclear shield i.e., Nuclear Missile Defence (NMD). Heavy investment in AD Systems has become mandatory as deep strike aircraft with BVR nuclear strikes and long-range missiles is a possibility. Pakistan has an immature nuclear weapons doctrine; It is possible for terrorists sparking a tactical nuclear conflagration. India needs to invest in miniaturization of nuclear weapons as use of tactical weapons by Pakistan and China is a distinct possibility in the Tactical battle Area. Nations harbouring non-state actors have a shield of disclaimer that non-state actors or Taliban type rogue militia have caused an accident. ISIS is a good example of former military breaking into being militia fighters. This is possible in this region as US troops pulling out from Af - Pakistan area would trigger slip back of the region into being an epicentre of Global terrorism.[8] Similarly, China has been talking about local wars, if nuclear dimension is added to border wars it would be a dilemma for India to respond with *'massive retaliation' to a small use of a tactical nuclear bomb.*

Fusion bombs. These are thermonuclear weapons, a second-generation nuclear bomb design. Its greater sophistication affords it vastly greater destructive power than first-generation atomic bombs, a *more compact size, a lower mass or a combination of these benefits.* Characteristics of nuclear fusion reactions makes it possible for the use of non-fissile depleted uranium as the weapon's main fuel, thus allowing more efficient use of scarce fissile material such as uranium-235U or plutonium -239 (239

---

8   "Timeline: the Rise, Spread, and Fall of the Islamic State", Wilson Center, 28 October 2019, https://www.wilsoncenter.org/article/timeline-the-rise-spread-and-fall-the-islamic-state.

Pu). Modern fusion weapons consist essentially of two main components; a nuclear fission primary stage (fuelled by 235U or 239Pu) and a separate nuclear fusion secondary stage containing thermonuclear fuel; the heavy hydrogen isotopes deuterium and tritium, or in modern weapons - lithium deuteride. For this reason, thermonuclear weapons are often colloquially called hydrogen bombs or H-bombs. The amount of energy produced from fusion is very large, four times as much as nuclear fission reactions and fusion reactions can be the basis of future fusion power reactors. Plans call for first-generation fusion reactors to use a mixture of deuterium and tritium — heavy types of hydrogen. Fusion reactions take place in a state of matter called plasma — a hot, charged gas made of positive ions and free-moving electrons that have unique properties distinct from solids, liquids and gases. In theory, with just a few grams of these reactants, it is possible to produce a terajoule of energy, which is approximately the energy one person in a developed country needs over sixty years

Chemical Weapons. Such weapons use a chemical to cause intentional death or harm through its toxic properties covered under this category. It covers munitions, devices and other equipment fundamentally designed to weaponize toxic chemicals. *These weapons are easy to assemble, are highly cost effective, low tech, but cause serious damage therefore seen as poor man's WMD.* Chemical Weapons Convention (CWC) prohibits 'chemical weapons', it includes all toxic chemicals and their precursors, except when used for purposes permitted by the Convention – in quantities consistent with such a purpose. The full and legal definition of a Chemical Weapon can be found in Article II of the Chemical Weapons Convention.[9] The Convention defines each component of a chemical weapon as a chemical weapon — whether assembled or not, stored together or separately. Dual-use describes chemicals or equipment that can be used for peaceful civilian and commercial purposes, but can also be used in the creation of weapons or as weapons. The prohibition of the use of herbicides as a method of warfare is recognised in the CWC Preamble.

---

9   "What is a Chemical Weapon?", Organisation for the Prohibition of Chemical Weapons, https://www.opcw.org/our-work/what-chemical-weapon.

However, *herbicides are not defined specifically in the Convention.* Herbicides that are intentionally used to harm humans or animals through chemical action could be considered as a chemical weapon under the "general purpose criteria." Central Nervous System (CNS) - Acting Chemicals, which are sometimes referred to as incapacitating Chemical Agents (ICAs), are not defined or mentioned by name in the Convention. The definition of chemical weapons does not result in restrictions of any State Party's right to produce and use chemicals for peaceful purposes or to acquire and retain conventional weapons and their associated delivery systems. It is possible to synthesize many types of toxins in laboratories without harvesting the organisms that produce them in nature. Moreover, a number of toxins are also synthetic dual-use chemicals, meaning that under the CWC they can be produced in the quantities required for legitimate activities. Toxins are toxic chemicals produced by living organisms. These are considered as both chemical and biological weapons when used in violation of the Convention. The development, production and stockpiling of toxins for purposes of warfare are prohibited under both the CWC and Biological Weapons Convention (BWC). Types of Chemical Agents that can be used can be as choking agents, blister agents, blood agents and the less lethal Riot control agents. *The US forces in recent operations against Gaddafi in Libya recovered and destroyed 517 arty rounds with mustard.*[10] *We have a rogue Pakistan Army which is funded, enabled and uses all military tricks at their disposal, we need to build our defence mechanism against such rogue Chemical attacks.*

Radiological Weapons. Such weapons use radiating material specially with damaging rays to the human body or fissile material that can cause serious medical conditions leading to incapacitation or death. Radiation bomb is also called a dirty bomb that spreads radioactive material for mass disruption and not destruction. A nuclear detonation also creates a large burst of direct radiation but causes numerous blasts and burn injuries and

---

10 Eric Schmitt, "Libya's Cache of Toxic Arms All Destroyed", The New York Times, 2 February 2014, https://www.nytimes.com/2014/02/03/world/africa/libyas-cache-of-toxic-arms-all-destroyed.html.

disperse radioactive material widely (termed fallout). Radioactive material can be dispersed by packing it around a conventional explosive that is then detonated. People may also be exposed to radiation from a concealed source (for example, a container of radioactive material hidden in a public place such as under a subway). Doctors determine whether people have been exposed (irradiated), contaminated by radioactive dust and debris, or both. If contamination has occurred, doctors put people through decontamination measures.[11] Radioactive material can also be delivered by a drone, if gone undetected, the material can cause serious short and certain long-term incapacitation. These weapons are highly usable by non-state actors to cause panic in Hybrid war conditions. Radioactive isotopes also are considered as poor-man's bombs. Of these sources, only nine reactor produced isotopes stand out as being suitable for radiological terror: americium-241, californium-252, caesium-137, cobalt-60, iridium-192, plutonium-238, polonium-210, radium-226 and strontium-90. Therefore, detection of radiation is most important. Combat troops need to be equipped for reading the levels of radiological exposure and decontamination and treatment medicines.

EMP (Electromagnetic Pulse). EMP is an instantaneous, intense energy field that can overload or disrupt from a distance, numerous electrical systems and high technology microcircuits, which are especially sensitive to power surges. A large scale EMP effect can be produced by a single nuclear explosion detonated high in the atmosphere. This method is referred to as High-Altitude EMP (HEMP). A similar, smaller-scale EMP effect can be created using non-nuclear devices with powerful batteries or reactive chemicals. This method is called High Power Microwave (HPM). Several nations, including reported sponsors of terrorism, may currently have a capability to use EMP as a weapon for cyber warfare or cyber terrorism to disrupt communications. In the past, the threat of mutually assured destruction provided a lasting deterrent against the exchange of multiple high-yield nuclear warheads.

---

11 James M. Madsen, "Radiological Weapons", MSD Manual, February 2021, https://www.msdmanuals.com/en-in/professional/injuries-poisoning/mass-casualty-weapons/radiological-weapons.

However, now even a single, low-yield nuclear explosion high above or over a battlefield, can produce a large-scale EMP effect that could result in a widespread loss of electronics, but no direct fatalities, and may not necessarily evoke a large nuclear retaliatory strike. Policy issues raised by this threat include firstly, what are the nations doing to protect civilian critical infrastructure systems against the threat of EMP. Secondly, could the military be affected if an EMP attack is directed against the civilian infrastructure. Thirdly, are other nations now encouraged by EMP vulnerabilities to develop or acquire nuclear weapons, and fourthly, how likely are the terrorist organizations to launch a smaller-scale EMP attack. High Energy Attacks would initially complement and later supplement traditional kinetic energy attacks. These could be high lasers, high electronic beams and use of EM pulse. EMP weapons have been tried by China.[12] Such attacks are possible in counter space application as well, to neutralise the adversaries' military satellites through destruction or neutralising them.

Counter Space or the Anti-Satellite (ASAT). ASAT weapons are becoming intrinsic to Space Warfare. The space now becomes a rapidly contested global common, the space-faring nations are increasingly concerned about securing their space assets. It is assessed that soon every satellite in any orbit will be at risk from the Chinese ASAT weapons. China is building co-orbital counter-space capabilities which serve dual-purpose of inspection and on-orbit servicing during peacetime and could attack adversarial satellites during war.[13] It is claimed that India does not want to weaponize the space or create harmful debris. India has demonstrated its kinetic counter-space capability in March 2019 by shooting its own non-operational satellite in the Low Earth

---

12 Hercules Reyes, "China May Have Tested New Electromagnetic Weapon: Report", The Defense Post, 26 August 2021, https://www.thedefensepost.com/2021/08/26/china-new-electromagnetic-weapon/.

13 Mark Stokes, Gabriel Alvarado, Emily Weinstein, and Ian Easton, "China's Space and Counterspace Capabilities and Activities", The U.S.-China Economic and Security Review Commission, March 30, 2020, https://www.uscc.gov/sites/default/files/2020-05/China_Space_and_Counterspace_Activities.pdf.

Orbit.[14] India has several medium range and ICBMs that have the capability to deliver a credible payload into the orbit.

> **'Directed Energy'.** This is an important part of counter-space technology. The recent activities demonstrate that China is proliferating its electronic and cyber capabilities in space. In 2018 alone, China tested most technologies in the counterspace categories.[15] It is assessed that Chinese counter-space programmes are primarily designed to deter US strikes against China's space assets and deny superiority to the United States and even attack US satellites.[16] The US has been working on technology called satellite Melter, using redirecting solar beams to burn down the target satellites. Russia has Kinetic ASAT and co-orbital counter-space programmes. Russia's newest co-orbital system may be designed to target satellites in GEO. It is assessed to have the capability to destroy and degrade satellites using non-kinetic physical counter-space systems. Russia is likely capable of destructive cyber-warfare targeting satellite systems and the ground systems that support them.

> **Space based Second Strike.** These assets may be used to hold information, store high energy weapons as a deterrent and also ensure that the ability to respond is not destroyed by the adversary. Nations are investing hugely in Space labs and large facilities. It would be possible for Space faring nations to build space arsenals for mass destruction meant for a second strike and to act as additional redundancy. However, such assets will need protection in the space that would happen through miniaturization and strong defensive and hardened assets.

---

14 Ashley J. Tellis, "India's ASAT Test: An Incomplete Success", Carnegie Endowment for International Peace, 15 April 2019, https://carnegieendowment.org/2019/04/15/india-s-asat-test-incomplete-success-pub-78884.

15 Mark Stokes, Gabriel Alvarado, Emily Weinstein, and Ian Easton, "China's Space and Counterspace Capabilities and Activities", no. 72

16 Ibid.

LAWS (Lethal Autonomous Weapons). LAWS are a type of autonomous military system that can independently search and engage targets based on programmed constraints and descriptions. LAWS are highly sophisticated autonomous military weapon systems with an array of sensor suites and pre-programmed computer algorithms which can independently search, select, designate, track, engage and eliminate hostile targets. These weapon systems, once activated, can destroy targets without further human intervention. Hence LAWS on a broad scale can transform the structure of war by bringing in Artificial Intelligence (AI) into systems governing weapons, where humans would remain out of the loop. The AI-triggered Revolution in Military Affairs (RMA) is happening in the leading military establishments across the world. Fully-autonomous defensive systems have already been deployed by many advanced countries to intercept air aggression. Defensive weapon systems are deployed to seek all incoming aerial targets. The most common autonomous defensive weaponry is the Missile Defence Systems (MDS).[17] Both the US and Israel have deployed and tested MDS successfully. Fire-and-forget systems have been deployed by both the UK and Israel. Even South Korea uses the SGR-A1, a sentry robot with an automatic mode, in the demilitarised border zone with North Korea.[18] Norway has an offensive autonomous system which will be deployed under the Joint Strike Missile program of NATO. This system can hunt, recognize and detect a target ship or land-intervention. Both Russia and China are developing similar systems at a faster pace.

Air Power. This is a more traditional means of ISR and to deliver stand-off strikes. The Gulf wars demonstrated the role of

---

17 Comdr Jayakrishnan N Nair, "Lethal Autonomous Weapon Systems – A Challenge to Humanity", Indian Defence Review, 9 April 2020, http://www.indiandefencereview.com/news/lethal-autonomous-weapon-systems-a-challenge-to-humanity/

18 Alexander Velez-Green, "The Foreign Policy Essay: The South Korean Sentry—A "Killer Robot" to Prevent War", Lawfare, 1 March 2015, https://www.lawfareblog.com/foreign-policy-essay-south-korean-sentry%E2%80%94-killer-robot-prevent-war.

Airpower which was the sole demonstrator of precision targeting. Taking a leaf from the Gulf War, China started building its Air Force for air dominance. PLAAF today is the second biggest air force in the world, whereas IAF is the fourth largest. PLAAF has a long-range strategic bomber fleet and holds large strategic assets such as airborne warning and control system (AWACS) aircraft and combat drones compared with the IAF. The PLAAF operates Su-30MKK and MK2 all-weather, long-range strike fighters. The PLAAF has an operational force of at least 200 fifth generation and 600 fourth-generation fighters including J-10B/C, J-11B, J-16, and Su-30.[19] It has also forayed into the development of fifth-generation fighters such as J-20 and FC-31/J-31. The IAF's induction of Rafale fighters, which are typically 4.5 generation fighters will enable it to maintain air superiority over China's J10, J11, and Su-27 fighter jets. Armed with Meteor very long-range and MICA beyond visual range (BVR) air-to-air missiles, the Rafale fighters are expected to pose a significant threat to Chinese aerial assets. Sukhoi Su-30MKI serves the IAF as the primary air superiority fighter with the capability to perform air-to-ground strike missions. The IAF operates more than 270 Su-30MKIs and is fielding HAL Tejas, the fourth-generation multirole light fighter to replace its ageing MiG-21 interceptor aircraft. The IAF fleet includes all-weather MiG-29 multi-role aircraft and Jaguar all-weather attack aircraft.[20]

Although the PLAAF has started inducting J-20, which was claimed to be a fifth-generation fighter for its stealth features, it is believed to be not superior to IAF Rafale, a 4.5-generation aircraft.[21] In case of a high-altitude war, India is better placed than China as many of the IAF aircraft are capable of flying at high altitudes

---

19 Ajay, "India vs China: Airpower compares", Airforce Technology, 31 July 2020, https://www.airforce-technology.com/features/india-vs-china-indian-air-force-iaf-vs-peoples-liberation-army-air-force-plaaf/.

20 Ritesh K Srivastava, "IAF's lethal flying machines that give India an 'edge' over Pakistan, China", Zee News, 22 September 2020, https://zeenews.india.com/photos/india/iaf-s-lethal-flying-machines-that-give-india-an-edge-over-pakistan-china-2311493.

21 Ajay, "India vs China: Airpower compares", no. 78

in all-weather conditions with support from nearby airbases.[22] PLAAF aircraft may have to fly with limited supplies and fuel due to rough weather conditions in their airbases near Tibet. China has been, however, developing military airfields in Tibet since the last decade and has significantly enhanced the ground facilities for the operation of PLAAF's combat aircraft.

China's bomber force comprises the H-6 Badger bomber variants. The Xian H-6K bomber is capable of carrying six land-attack cruise missiles (LACMs) providing the PLAAF with a long-range, precision-strike capability to target any part of India.[23] The IAF, on the other hand, has no strategic bomber fleet and limited options to deploy its AN-32 transport aircraft and multi-role fighters in bombing missions.[24] India's state-of-the-art strategic air lifters, including the C-17 and C-130J, Ilyushin Il-76, Antonov An-32, and Dornier Do 228 ensure rapid transfer of equipment and supplies to air bases near the LAC, which is the need of the hour for ground forces on the battlefield. The PLAAF's comparatively smaller fleet of strategic airlift assets includes Y-20 large transport aircraft and Russian-made Il-76 aircraft.

As of December 2020, the only combat-ready stealth aircraft in service are the 5th generation fighters Northrop Grumman B-2 Spirit (1997), the Lockheed Martin F-22 Raptor (2005); the Lockheed Martin F-35 Lightning II (2015; the Chengdu J-20 (2017), and the Sukhoi Su-57 (2020), with a number of other countries developing their own design to innovate extra stealthy bombers to replace B-2/B-52. Sixth-gen fighters will be defined by several new technologies, including just one large transmitter that acts as an air-to-air radar, air-to-ground radar, radio, and electronic warfare platform. A single system controlled by software would replace several different systems, switching between tasks as needed. The Raytheon sixth-gen fighters being developed will

---

22 "How India military stacks up vis-a-vis Chinese defence forces", Hindustan Times, 19 June 2020, https://www.hindustantimes.com/india-news/how-india-military-stacks-up-vis-a-vis-chinese-defence-forces/story-OHXDNM1X3al4DBSohTgZRI.html.

23 Ibid.

24 Ibid.

also include self-landing systems, land autonomously on land and aircraft carriers, which could be used to land the aircraft in rough weather at a "precise landing zone." A sixth-gen fighter could land autonomously, without human control, or provide guidance to pilots landing under challenging circumstances. The US aerospace industry has carried out a number of successful trials to convert from manned aircraft to unmanned - Robot Pilot. The fighter plane shall be able to fly and fight while being controlled by a robot. The cockpit design is such that the AI driven pilot box is fitted in place of a pilot in the cockpit. Once fielded, all current generation fighting machines would be converted into autonomous flying machines making air engagements more risk averse.

IAF also employs combat-proven aerial platforms such as AH-64E Apache and CH-47F Chinook ensure reliability during conflicts, HAL Light Combat Helicopters (LCH) and HAL Rudra attack helicopters are dedicated for combat missions. AH-64E Apache attack helicopters will enable the IAF to perform day/night, all-weather attack missions especially in rugged mountain regions of India-China borders. The PLAAF operates the WZ-10 attack helicopters, Mil Mi-8, and Harbin Z-9 utility helicopters, and Changhe Z-8 transport/utility helicopters.

A large UAV fleet works to PLAAF's advantage in conducting sorties and strikes near the borders with no risk of damage to their manned aircraft and crew. The PLAAF operates Yunying (CloudShadow) armed reconnaissance unmanned aerial vehicles (UAVs), Gongji 1 armed intelligence, surveillance and reconnaissance (ISR) UAVs, CH-4 and CH-5, and Yilong (Wing Loong) series of unmanned aircraft, which can carry two or more air-to-surface guided munitions. The IAF, on the other hand, deploys a smaller UAV fleet that includes IAI Searcher II and IAI Heron for reconnaissance and surveillance missions. India plans to buy 30 armed MQ-9B Predator drones from the U.S.[25] to boost its sea and land defence. The deal would add to

---

25 Sudhi Ranjan Sen, "India to buy 30 US Predator drones for $3 bn to counter China, Pakistan", Business Standard, 11 March 2021, https://www.business-standard.com/article/current-affairs/india-to-buy-30-us-predator-drones-for-3-bn-to-counter-china-pakistan-121031000515_1.html.

India's military capabilities as the drones it has now can only be used for surveillance and reconnaissance. Drones can be used in combination of space for better communication, control and recce. The satellite images can be used as tandem imageries being taken by drones at the same time for enhancing redundancy and resolution of pictures. Similarly, sensor shooter combination with space adds to a precision punch.

Air-launched Rapid Response Weapon (ARRW). ARRW is being developed by the U.S. The Air Force is yet to conduct a successful live-fire test of its new AGM-183, but says that it has now simulated the entire "kill chain" for employing one of these hypersonic missiles.[26] With no actual weapon fired, the networks used to send the targeting information may be the more significant capability demonstrated. Developed by Lockheed Martin, the boost glide weapon is propelled to a maximum speed of Mach 7 + by a missile before gliding towards its target. A B-52 Stratofortress bomber from the 49th Test and Evaluation Squadron, based at Barksdale Air Force Base in Louisiana, served as the launch platform, though no weapon was actually released. The designated target was 600 nautical miles from the bomber at the time of the simulated AGM-183A launch. The Air Force said that the test had been carried out "in the highly contested and realistic threat environment that Northern Edge, Alaska provides."

Naval Power. The Navy has been traditionally significant but with modernisation and expansion of the PLA Navy, China is threatening to establish supremacy, and has created a new contest of Islands and dominance of oceans. This integrates the Anti Access/ Area Denial (A2/AD) strategy meant to prevent an adversary from occupying or traversing an area of land, sea or air. The Chinese ships, aircraft and weapons are now comparable in many respects to those of Western navies. The PLA Navy is reported to have more than 300 surface combatants, submarines, amphibious ships, patrol craft and other specialized vessels. The US Navy has 293 ships with

---

26 Joseph Trevithick, "B-52 Simulated A Hypersonic Weapon Strike During Massive Alaskan War Games", The Drive, 6 May 2021, https://www.thedrive.com/the-war-zone/40494/b-52-simulated-a-hypersonic-weapon-strike-during-massive-alaskan-war-games.

an aim to increase the fleet to 355 vessels, but with a change in the mix of the fleet architecture such as unmanned systems.[27] It is expected the PLA navy will continue to surpass the U.S. Navy in the number of warships built for the foreseeable future.[28] The United States currently has 11 nuclear-powered aircraft carriers, and is acquiring new Ford-class platforms, which are designed to enable a 33 percent increase in sortie generation rate. The US plans to deploy stealthy, fifth-generation F-35C fighter jets on its carriers, as well as an unmanned aerial tanker MQ-25 Stingray. China currently has only two carriers. A third Chinese carrier is under construction, and a fourth may begin construction as early as 2021.[29] These future vessels are likely to be equipped with electromagnetic catapults rather than a ski ramp, which will improve the range and payload capability of the fixed-wing aircraft. China reportedly plans to develop a carrier-capable variant of its J-20 or FC-31 fifth-generation stealth fighters, as well as a carrier-based stealth drone. By 2035, we shall witness projection through a large number of warships in Indo Pacific with new technology. Trials are being conducted for drone planes where every ship can be an aircraft carrier - have a drone plane onboard that takes off as a drone and flies like a plane.

The US Navy currently has 69 submarines. It recently signed a contract for a block buy of nine Virginia-class, nuclear-powered attack submarines that will be equipped with the Virginia Payload Module to boost each vessel's Tomahawk cruise missile carrying capacity by about 75 percent.[30] It is also pursuing a new class of 12 nuclear-powered ballistic missile subs, the Columbia, to replace

---

27 Jon Harper, "Eagle vs Dragon: How the U.S. and Chinese Navies Stack Up", National Defense, 3 September 2020, https://www.nationaldefensemagazine. org/articles/2020/3/9/eagle-vs-dragon-how-the-us-and-chinese-navies-stack-up.

28 Ibid.

29 "China's next aircraft carrier likely nuclear powered, says report", Aljazeera, 13 March 2021, https://www.aljazeera.com/news/2021/3/13/chinas-next-aircraft-carrier-could-be-nuclear-powered-report.

30 "Navy Force Structure and Shipbuilding Plans: Background and Issues for Congress", Congressional Research Service, 3 August 2021, https://sgp.fas. org/crs/weapons/RL32665.pdf.

the aging Ohio class. China's submarines are armed with anti-ship cruise missiles, wire-guided and wake-homing torpedoes, and mines, and each Jin-class boat is expected to be armed with 12 JL-2 nuclear-armed ballistic missiles. With new production facilities, China may soon be able to launch two SSNs and one SSBNs annually, giving it as many as 24 SSNs and 14 SSBNs by 2030. Beijing "remains engaged in a robust surface combatant construction program, producing new guided-missile cruisers (CG), guided-missile destroyers (DDG) and guided-missile frigates (FFG) which will significantly upgrade the PLA Navy's air defence, anti-ship and anti-submarine capabilities."[31]

Platforms are not the only part of the equation when it comes to measuring naval power, weapon systems enabled by sensors, communications networks, well-trained sailors and sound operating concepts are also critical. China and the United States are both developing and fielding new missiles and other advanced weaponry, and the race is on to see who can pack the most punch. The US claims that it has fielded a low-yield, submarine-launched ballistic missile nuclear warhead, the W76-2, on its boomers. Other next-generation weapons, such as directed energy, are likely to be added to the fleet.

US and Chinese navies are beefing up their weapons arsenals to avoid being outgunned China is believed to be fielding advanced anti-ship ballistic missiles, including the Dong Feng-26 with a maximum range of about 2,160 nautical miles. There are concerns about China's ASBMs, because such missiles, in combination with broad-area maritime surveillance and targeting systems would enable China to attack adversaries' aircraft carriers.[32] Beijing's military also has an extensive inventory of anti-ship cruise missiles including some advanced ones such as the YJ-18. The long ranges of certain Chinese ASCMs aim to Block 5 Tomahawks, a modified Standard Missile-6, the Long-Range Anti-Ship Missile and the

---

31 Jon Harper, "Eagle vs Dragon: How the U.S. and Chinese Navies Stack Up", no. 86

32 "China Naval Modernization: Implications for U.S. Navy Capabilities—Background and Issues for Congress", Congressional Research Service, 3 August 2021, https://sgp.fas.org/crs/row/RL33153.pdf.

Naval Strike Missile. Higher power lasers are finding relevance to add to the warfighting capability of ships. Both the U.S. and China are also working on game changing technology in hyper sonics to improve air- and underwater-launch testing capabilities for the conventional prompt strike program. There are plans to conduct flight tests of a hypersonic glide body this year.

Unmanned Naval Assets. These are incrementally being considered for deployment. It is known that the Chinese plan to develop an unmanned ship similar to the U.S. Navy's Sea Hunter.[33] Although the designation of the project is unknown, the trimaran is remarkably similar to the Sea Hunter in almost every respect. Based on imagery analysis, the builder and dimensions have been established. The un-crewed Sea Hunter has been designed under the 'Continuous Trail Unmanned Vessel' (ACTUV) program. The uncrewed surface vessel's (USV) primary mission is to track submarines. It is designed to "lock on" to a submarine and trail it continuously. Platforms of this size and with this autonomy may have additional capabilities. But the inference is that China may seek the same capability as the Navy's Sea Hunter. Due to their higher speed, nuclear-powered submarines could out-run the USV, so the US Navy's own submarine should be largely immune. But other countries in China's areas of interest such as Japan, Australia and India have diesel-electric submarines. Although manned platforms will remain a key component of navies, unmanned systems as the wave of the future. They are expected to be less expensive and keep sailors out of harm's way. Robotic vessels could be used for a variety of missions, including intelligence, surveillance and reconnaissance, and offensive strike operations. The US Navy is pursuing a family of small, medium and large unmanned surface vessels (USV) and unmanned underwater vessels (UUV). Some small UUVs are already in the fleet and operating today, and can be deployed from surface vessels for missions such as counter-mine warfare. UUVs are a few years ahead of USVs. Large robotics ships are expected to be fielded later

---

33 H I Sutton, "Chinese Navy Crafts Unmanned Sea Hunter Knock-off", USNI News, 25 September 2020, https://news.usni.org/2020/09/25/chinese-navy-crafts-unmanned-sea-hunter-knock-off.

in this decade. But more work remains to be done. Testing and experimentation with large USV prototypes like the Sea Hunter is ongoing. The platform has demonstrated the ability to sail from Hawaii to California.

While the naval modernization race between the United States and China has global implications, the biggest potential flashpoint is the Asia-Pacific, especially in the Western Pacific within the first and second island chains. In a conflict inside the first island chain, U.S. naval forces would also generally have much longer supply lines. "The U.S. is not going to find its way out of the current deepening naval confrontation with China. It will need a denial-oriented naval posture in the Asia-Pacific and a higher level of technological specialisation.

Air Defence (AD). AD is gaining prominence as the aerial platforms are getting smarter, stealthier and faster. Air or Aerospace Defence provides a secure foundation for the safe and effective launch of aircraft and missiles to tackle an airborne or space-based intruder. Besides, the sharp end comprising aircraft, missiles and air defence guns, the first to detect intruders are the radars. The radars, along with an efficient Command, Control and Communication system, form a comprehensive Air Defence Network.[34] In our context, there are natural questions; Is the surveillance network in the Indian airspace gap-free? Is there adequate overlap between low, medium and high levels of radar coverage? The answer is obvious that we need a comprehensive radar coverage including Airborne Warning and control Systems (AWACS). Low level warning radars are important to detect cruise and hypersonic missiles. Even advanced Air Defence missiles such as S-400/500, Iron Dome, Barak missiles, need protection against Hypersonic missiles. The arrangements have to be based on hybrid radar plus satellite systems to detect hypersonic missiles and hit them with speed and accuracy.

---

34 Air Marshal Raghu Rajan, "Defending the Indian Skies", Indian Defence Review, 22 October 2012, http://www.indiandefencereview.com/spotlights/defending-the-indian-skies/.

The PLAAF enjoys the advantage of holding long-range air defence systems, which can defend potential aerial threats from the IAF. Further, long-range surface-to-air defence systems including S-300 and S-400 ensure the PLAAF to counter incoming aircraft, UAVs and cruise missiles from India. The PLAAF holds one of the world's largest inventories of advanced long-range surface-to-air missile (SAM) systems incorporated into SA-20 battalions imported from Russia and indigenously-produced CSA-9 (HQ-9) battalions.[35] With the S-400 Triumf SAM system in its arsenal, the PLAAF can intercept incoming aerial targets at a range of 400km, ensuring superior air defence capabilities against India. India holds an inventory of air defence missile systems which can engage targets within the range of 100km. The IAF's SAM inventory includes S-125 Pechora, 9K33 Osa-AK, 9K38 Igla-1, Akash, and SPYDER, Barak 8 missile defence systems. India has ordered the S-400 Triumf SAM system to make its air defence stronger against potential air attacks from neighbours.

While making skies safe, it is important to have counter to smart attack systems such as Suter Airborne Attack System, it hacks into the air defence systems so that they can be taken over. Suter includes some powerful sensors for detecting a large-scale assortment of electronic emissions, taking control of the enemy networks by manipulating the sensors.

BMD (Ballistic Missile Defence). BMD systems are based on the same principles as the AD, however, with a mix of ICBMs and shorter-range missiles, it is important to identify the missile threat right from the time it is launched. This is an area where not much information is available in the public domain. The requirement is to detect the launch and track the movement of ballistic missiles during their passage in space and when they re-enter the atmosphere, to home on to the target. This requires a series of space-based radars to cover the areas of interest and to have special ground-based ones which will take over the task of

---

35 Amrita Nayak Dutta, "Satellite images reveal China is building surface-to-air missile site at Mansarovar Lake", The Print, 20 August 2020, https://theprint. in/defence/satellite-images-reveal-china-is-building-surface-to-air-missile-site-at-mansarovar-lake/486091/.

tracking missiles as they enter its coverage area, then launch anti-ballistic measures to effect successful intercept. It is possible to use submarine launched/aircraft launched anti-ballistic missiles too.

Similarly, drones are increasingly becoming aerial intruders which can be used for multifarious purposes. Being a very small and versatile target, it is difficult to engage a full range of drones. The multi spectrum frequency waves would be necessary to disrupt the drone command and control links. It would be necessary to deploy anti-drone surveillance drones constantly flying sentry sorties and then have defensive drones destroying intruding drones.

Anti-Detection and Protection Systems. Such systems are becoming increasingly necessary for survival which is the most important aspect of warfare. If one cannot be detected one cannot be hit. Stealth technologies are being used such as *anti-radiation paints and materials* to avoid detection by radars and electronic cameras to defeat the adversary's ISR. China has been building underground facilities and related infrastructure to ensure their logistics bases, missile sites and military hardware in concentration areas are not picked up by satellite images.[36] Subterranean domain extends to Naval power where conventional ships especially big aircraft carriers would be easy targets of Space controlled missiles, therefore, more and more Navies in the world are investing in silent nuclear powered submarines, which have longer radius of operations as they can stay underwater for months.

Since swarm drones are increasingly being used for operational and tactical surveillance, anti-drone technology like laser and high frequency wave cannons are being fielded to deny surveillance and defend attacks from drones. Quantum stealth - Hyper stealth technology (Hides infrared, ultraviolet and thermal signals) combined with unpredictability of direction of attack is increasingly shaping the defence and attack technologies. Such technologies can be called *'perfect Signature management'* so

---

36 Detresfa, Sim Track, The Intel Lab, Tyler Rogoway, "Tracking China's Sudden Airpower Expansion On Its Western Border", The Drive, 16 June 2021, https://www.thedrive.com/the-war-zone/41065/tracking-chinas-sudden-airpower-expansion-along-its-western-border.

that assets are unidentifiable by all modern surveillance and identification systems.

DARPA has been working on imaginative technologies to enhance survival of underwater surveillance or reconnaissance vehicles, by making robots appear to look like fish using bio-technology. Similarly, these innovations are motivating the companies to produce combat robots in the shape of an animal.

Plasma Protection 'Force Field' has developed a force field-like system that can protect military platforms from shockwaves following from missiles or improvised explosive devices. This works through a combination of lasers, electricity and microwaves to rapidly heat up the air between the vehicle and the blast that would detect and absorb energy from incoming shockwaves to protect vehicles and critical Vulnerable Points.

Part III: Contact: Kinetic

'Contact Wars' are likely to transform dramatically, since these involve enormous human effort and risk. Technology would ensure that soldiers in the frontline are more at ease, have better protective and survival equipment and have better situational awareness. *'Manned borders' would be replaced with 'smart borders'*, giving the border guarding units sufficient time to react and defend a piece of territory under threat. Soldiers would be more mobile, and supported with autonomous weapons having a capability of first response. The border guarding forces need to transform to Border Surveillance Forces manning *digital borders* with deep warning systems giving enough time for the punitive forces to respond.

Infantry. The infantry Soldier, would be armed with light, wearable surveillance and weapon controlling devices. He would have the option of firing a weapon himself or directing a weapon system to fire which is deployed in offset / mounted configuration. These weapons would have the capability of firing steerable bullets and projectiles. Robotic systems are likely to be an important part of the mix of future ground-based warfighting capabilities and key contributors to reducing the risks to troops by improving sensing and targeting, reducing the danger of collateral damage. The boots on ground would reduce as gradually the robotics and AI powered soldiers shall replace human involvement. There will, however, be a need for some 'boots on the ground' in case there is a need to interact with the local population. All engagement decisions will have a 'human in the loop' hence these would employ highly controlled autonomous weapons. Lasers and energy weapons could well become an important part of the whole defensive system. An Infantry soldier would have a luxury of assigning a robot buddy a more dangerous task of delivering a kinetic punch from a more exposed position. Robot buddies could be assigned to surveillance and vanguard duties. Soldiers would increasingly be equipped with Artificial Intelligent wearables and implants that would increase awareness and give them mental and physical augmentation.

Special Forces (SF). These need to achieve undetected penetration behind enemy lines. Carry out stealth operations for a prolonged period to include recce and direction action tasks and exfiltrate rapidly. The western armies are trying Flyboard Air insertion which is still in the trial stage but seems promising. The Delta Force used a deadly combination of strategic electronic surveillance, snipers and drones armed with hellfire missiles to eliminate Iran's most powerful military commander Qassem Soleimani. SF carries out the most dangerous missions in the world, increasingly in hybrid scenarios, and would need rapid switch to high technology for high impact and low signature operations that guarantees mission success and high survivability.

Protracted Engagements. These would be a norm in Hybrid war scenarios. There would be few periods of peace due to fatigueless intervention by technology in military and public life. The security agencies and systems would need round the clock vigil in all spheres. Due to the continuous state of security alerts, nations, if not already engaged, would need to remain prepared for war. This perpetual engagement could mount expenses and make warfare unaffordable and unstainable. Nations would have no option but devising means to fight economical wars. That is how sub-conventional and Hybrid Wars came to being a 'Low-cost option'. Even though *future warfare would have fewer contact battles, there would be battles nonetheless.* All weapons would add lethality, accuracy, and range. Tanks, Artillery guns and drones would be all pervasive, inter-connected, made lighter, amphibious, multi terrain/ multidimensional, autonomous with high precision strike capability. Heavy armour would be replaced with Active protection systems that can destroy or mitigate incoming fire, or use novel materials that combine high protection with low weight, thereby boosting vehicle speed and agility.

Unmanned and Autonomous Systems. Vehicles, aircraft and ships would see a larger role in the battlefield. The pilotless, driver less or crew less fighting machines would be pervasive. The control stations of these machines could be located underground and far away from the War Zone. Such machines would be remotely controlled through secure and stable cable, radio and satellite communication which are uninterruptible, reliable and instant. The ranges or the radius of action and stamina of these machines would be enhanced through efficient power of hybrid engines requiring low maintenance or charging. The warheads could be Kinetic, High Energy or Radiological. Nuclear power would run engines in miniature plants that would empower these killing machines. These vehicles could be light in weight, smaller in size yet having the ability to carry on themselves disproportionate loads. The rearming and refuelling, if and when required, could be executed through an autonomous logistic support system.

Stealth Technologies. These with novel drive systems that reduce engine heat signatures could also enhance survivability without the need to build on more metal, by making tomorrow's tanks and AFVs harder to detect and more difficult to hit. The future battlefield would see unmanned armoured ground vehicles playing their part as we target greater automation which has made it possible for drones to have remotely controlled unmanned turrets. This trend is likely to continue grow towards *deployment a ground swarm of drone vehicles* in support of conventional MBTs and AFVs. Tanks would be empowered with massively enhanced situational awareness sensors, high-speed electro-hybrid drive and mounted laser emitters. Developments in light, high-capacity batteries will play as much a part in light, effective armour. The technology is becoming available to take a very different approach to MBT design using advanced materials, novel automotive systems, new weapon systems and active protection systems, resulting in much lighter, more agile platforms. "There will always be the issue of affordability and robustness that comes with increased complexity, as these advanced solutions must be able to operate reliably in all environments and be resilient to all types of terrain and threat."[1]

---

1   "What does the future hold for tanks?", Army Technology, 2 January 2017,

The Tank Boats concept based on the Indonesia model would be highly effective for beach operations and also for defending territories based on lakes such as Pangong Tso lake. The weapon system has the base of a boat and hull and turret of a tank.

Artillery. The artillery would improve Recce Surveillance and Target Acquisition (RSTA) by automation providing the army with exceptional battlefield capabilities, both by day and night. Satellites and UAVs have revolutionised RSTA. Precision Guidance Munition (PGM),[2] also called smart weapons, smart munitions, smart bombs would precisely hit a specific target. Long-range, quick response, surface-to-surface Tactical Missile Systems would be effective, against mobile and other targets and would gradually replace guns. This would include the Brilliant Anti-Armour/Tank (BAT) submunition. The self-guided, anti-armour Javelin missile's success was due to the two-dimensional arrays which made the missile's seeker almost foolproof. Other developments in inertial navigation are the Precision Inertial Navigation Systems (PINS), Micro inertial navigation technology (MINT) and Chip-scale atomic clock program (CSAC). PINS is an effort to address the vulnerabilities of GPS.

The US Army has developed Precision Guidance Kit (PGK) and Excalibur, as well as the Advanced Precision Mortar Initiative (APMI—GPS guidance for 120 mm mortars) and the Very Affordable Precision Projectile (VAPP) to increase precision strike.[3] The PGK replaces the fuse in the nose of conventional 155-mm artillery. PGK provides a Circular Error of Probability of 50m for all ranges, depending on the type of ammunition being fired. PGMs need a reliable power supply thus another area of

---

https://www.army-technology.com/features/featurewhat-does-the-future-hold-for-tanks-5688047/.

2   Lt. Gen. Naresh Chand (Retd), "Artillery Employment and Future Technologies", SP's Land Forces, Issue 5, 2017, https://www.spslandforces.com/story/?id=471&h=Artillery-Employment-and-Future-Technologies.

3   Kyle Mizokami, "The US Army Is Developing Artillery That Has GPS Precision—Without GPS", Popular Mechanics, 10 April 2018, https://www.popularmechanics.com/military/weapons/a19735395/the-us-army-is-developing-artillery-that-has-gps-precisionwithout-gps/.

development is to provide reliable and small sized batteries which have a long shelf life. The future PGM would be able to operate in any environment, with or without GPS and be able to change the type of explosion to match the target.

The Indian Army (IA) is procuring Raytheon Missile developed M982 Excalibur precision-guided artillery shells from the US.[4] These 155mm/52-cal shells will be used for M-777 field howitzers and the K-9 Vajra self-propelled howitzers. Excalibur is considered as a true precision weapon, impacting at a radial miss distance of less than two meters from the target. Indian Army in the past utilized the Russian Krasnopol 155mm laser-guided shells. For area targets, a torrent of inexpensive shells provide for a variety of weapons and shell types. GPS guided artillery shells are probably more suitable for larger calibre weapons where their low rate of fire would be compensated for with first shot precision, but for lighter weapons where rate of fire can compensate for the lighter projectile, precision will mean they can engage more targets and their lighter weight, capable in shoot and scoot roles. Shaped charges tend to derive their penetration from their diameter, so a 155mm/52 calibre is better at penetrating than a smaller calibre. Smaller circuit cards and enhanced shock protection for electronics made guidance achievable for the M982 Excalibur artillery shell.

Missiles. These can be used for better accuracy such as 'Beyond line-of-sight' fire. With missiles in the canister, can be vertically launched, with a command and control system in a box. It can be mounted on a truck, or set up on the ground. The Non-Line-of-Sight Launch System (NLOS-LS) can be utilized in the Unmanned Surface Vehicle or in the Navy's Littoral Combat Ship. NLOS-LS has two missiles, first, a Precision Attack Missile (PAM) with high speed to hit targets at maximum range. The second one would be a

---

4   Debajit Sarkar, "M982 Excalibur Precision Guided Artillery Shells: Everything you need to know about true precision weapon", Financial Express, 25 October 2019, https://www.financialexpress.com/defence/m982-excalibur-precision-guided-artillery-shells-everything-you-need-to-know-about-true-precision-weapon/1745798/.

Loitering Attack Missile (LAM), equipped with laser detection and ranging ("Ladar") seeker, can achieve a range of 70 Kms and then a 30-minute loiter time. It is able to loiter over targets of interest, do automatic target recognition and attack targets on its own.

Enhancement of Lethality and Precision. This is also enhanced with more advanced systems such as Explosively formed jets (EFJ) and self-forging penetrators (SFP) used for precision strike against targets such as armoured vehicles and reinforced structures. The Magneto Hydrodynamic Explosive Munition (MAHEM) programme can achieve higher efficiency by using a compressed magnetic flux generator (CMFG) - driven magneto hydro-dynamically formed metal jets and SFP with significantly improved performance over EFJ. To enhance the rapid-fire capability of an artillery shell, Multi-**Azimuth Defence — Fast Intercept Round Engagement System (MAD-FIRES).** These would combine precision and manoeuvrability to alter their flight path in real time to stay on target and a capacity to continuously target, track and engage multiple fast-approaching targets simultaneously and re-engage any targets that survive initial engagement. High Explosive Guided Mortar (HEGM) provides integral indirect fire mortar munitions to Infantry and Special Operations units. The XM395 will engage targets as close as 500m-6,500m threshold and 1,000 m-15000m objective. Some more examples of current PGMs are:

> **M712 Copperhead.** This has a laser guided projectile, fired from a 155mm gun with a maximum range of 16 km. Copperhead operates in two modes. Ballistic and Glide modes depending on the visibility.

> **M898 155mm Sense and Destroy Armour (SADARM).** The shell has a nose-mounted M762/ M767 fuse set to burst at 1,000 m above the target for releasing two SADARM submunitions, ejected from the projectile with the help of parachutes. Each sensor with the submunitions has a milli-meter radiometer which scans an area of 150m in diameter, tracks and guides the submunition onto the target.

> **XM395 Precision Guided Mortar Munition (PGMM)** combines GPS guidance and directional control, transforming existing 120mm mortar bombs into PGMs with a CEP of 5m at a range of 7000m.

Attack Helicopters (AH). These are considered as the manoeuvre arm of the Army. AHs are also referred to as flying Battle Tanks or the third dimensional armour and are incrementally adding high speeds, agility and protection. They are armed with mixed arsenal such as guided missiles, rockets, cannons and guns shooting at rapid and cyclical rates. They have excellent surveillance, navigation, protection and communication systems on board. Apache AH-64E (I) helicopters have been recently inducted into the IAF, has the fastest rate of climb making it more agile in the battlefield with the ability to fight in Altitudes upto 21000 ft. The AH-64E is an advanced multi-mission helicopter with the latest technology insertions, maintaining its standing as the world's best attack helicopter. Suitable to be employed against China's WZ-10 which has a slower rate of climb, a disadvantage in steep mountain ranges of Aksai Chin - Eastern Ladakh area. The nearest comparable AH with AH-64E(I) is the Russian Ka 52 kamov. Kamov 50/52 is more suited for lower hills/ plains with marginally higher speed and range than AH-64.

Part IV: Technology Enablers and Future

Artificial Intelligence (AI). AI using the power of 'Data' is another name of machine intelligence, where computers use data to analyse, process and provide machine logic. Machines initially supported by humans would acquire data and write algorithms. This process becomes cyclic where humans would be replaced by machines that would operate neural networks by writing their own algorithms and run programs intended to deliver the end result in an 'autonomous manner'. The machines would self-learn and operate cognitive networks powered by sensors. Since machines would replace humans, the *first field of jobs handed over to the machine would be the most dangerous job - a job of a soldier and gradually military as a profession would largely be outsourced to the domain of Robots.*

Robotics. These would be seen as the major game changer in the medium to long term. Artificial Intelligence would power machines and humans in a major way. This would accelerate all processes of growth and economy but also trigger a sharp divide between humanity. A side that is powered with AI and Robotics, even though smaller in number, would be 'haves' and shall dominate the other part not having access to this 'virtual power' would remain 'have nots' - left completely outmatched. In a contest or a clash in any field, likely to become a routine way of business, shall make 'have nots' literal slaves to the 'neo-colonists' - the halves.

Autonomous Systems. They would in more than many ways replace human beings. To begin with, as discussed, all the dangerous or subhuman jobs would be outsourced to these intelligent machines. AI would soon be seen as the *largest outsourcing ever witnessed in global history.* AI engines are double edged, super-productive or super-destructive - when not regulated or controlled. The first shift is likely to happen in the security business, starting from personal, home, community or even National Security. The Autonomous systems powered by the machine would not only replace the fighting machines, making planes, tanks, guns and the military machinery autonomous. Making sure there is no risk to a human in warfighting. Even the frontline fighting soldier would be a Robot in the privileged Forces. The AI driven military machines would be mainly employed for grabbing or protecting resources, such as water, rare and precious minerals on earth and planets, and/or taking down the industrial potential of adversaries. The side which does not employ such machines would remain defenceless and capitulate or surrender. This process, in a manner, has already begun. Economy and Technology are now seen as the main ingredients of *Comprehensive National Power*. Nations rich in both, have started enslaving the others.

Digital Technology. This is the mother of all technologies. AI power cannot be realised unless nations invest rightly in digital platforms. Security of AI platforms would be of prime concern not only for the military application but for all critical infrastructure of the nation such as power grids, airlines, banking systems, strategic industry etc. The investments must be prioritised into making national budgets where the digital industry gets an urgent and a larger chunk of the pie. The governments must see the urgency in such financial allocations since survival of the nation would largely depend on how urgently you implement technology. The transformation is needed in turning the analogous systems into autonomous systems, both for critical infrastructure as well as military. The AI engines would enable them to be networked as swarms and self-assign targets between machines. Networks will make it possible to build H-M2M-H (Human-Machine to Machine-Human) interfaces to bring battles to be planned, regulated and controlled from manned war rooms, yet fought by machines in the field.

Science and Technology. This remains a baseline for technological growth. China outlined a list of sixteen megaprojects in the medium and long term Science and Technology Development Plan (2006-2020). The Chinese Ministry of Industry and Information

Technology issued a document on goals for the developing Artificial Intelligence from 2018 to 2020 in line with the vision of the top leadership for building a new Chinese economy in the age of AI. They aimed at China's ability to mass-produce neural-network processing chips by 2020. In 2018, Chinese President urged China to speed up its semiconductor strategy in the face of foreign pressure and growing demands on technology. China aims at reducing reliance on foreign technology by 2025. It has made a roadmap to make milestone contributions to the global scientific community by 2030 and ultimately be able to become the Science and Technology powerhouse by 2050.

Data. Data as they say is new oil. It is being constantly collected, stolen, spied on, analysed or even manipulated. Data is being sold at huge costs from various agencies who come under the garb of innocent service providers. These companies offer so many freebies that a customer gets very tempted to buy the product such as Apps, games and instant global connection. Increasingly, these companies are collaborating or buying others out so that the data sample size becomes larger making the machines use the raw data as fodder for analytics and deep learning. The machines can process huge amounts of data in a matter of seconds and establish a 'cause and effect' relationship and make quick comparative analysis. The Machines shorten the OODA (Observe Orient Decide and Act) loop to a mere instant process. The speed and accuracy of decision making can beat the competitor hands down. Side which employs smarter and faster machines would win the 'first draw' engagements instantly. Conversely, if the adversary employs machines with inferior technology or has inadequate data would instantly make slower and inaccurate assessment therefore fall behind in the OODA cycle. Worst would be a case of an inferior adversary who does possess data or not use machines at all, or has machines with low data in it or even worse is when in spite of having both, it allows its data to be manipulated. Such disruption would cause instant loss to the weaker adversaries in all forms of engagement, whether it is trade, commerce, targeting critical infrastructure and even war.

Indian Industry. Our Defence industry needs an urgent re-orientation. To be able to absorb the AI into all our systems including national security apparatus, industry cannot rely on imported chips / semiconductors. A large-scale communication network would be essential which is scalable and has 5G/6G capacities. Digitisation and indigenisation has to go hand in hand, right from designing to fabrication, all or most of it to be done on Indian soil. Indian industry has sufficient capacities to scale up ICT (Information and communication Technologies) provided the budgets and policies are supportive. In fact, ICT would be the main foundation to achieve digitisation, that would provide a baseline to create AI platforms. Data reservoirs would need early fruition to be able to get the machines to crank in the process of 'machine and deep learning'. Data management institutions would take time to come up. These must be built parallelly which might consume large manpower initially. India has a sizable IT and business base that would be able to shape up the Cyber domain in ensuring we build exclusive yet interactive domains.

AI has been adopted and used by the medical fraternity very appropriately, it helps in quick diagnosis by comparing data, it can make surgeons operate on patients who are located far away, even in remote areas. Specialists can write opinions and prescribe treatments through telemedicine. This technology is most rapidly advancing in military and aviation medicine. Indian Armed Forces have been able to create network telemedicine nodes across India. The electro-medical machines can be connected to computers to create virtual monitoring stations at multiple locations and seen by surgeons and surgeons sitting in super speciality hospitals, yet available to treat patients remotely. Similarly, other logistic support units can use AI for preventive maintenance, automatic inventory control, procurement and ensure that nation fights an efficient and economic war where there are no wasteful logistics,

India needs to strategically synergise with incubating technologies through the commercial domain such as start-ups into the ecosystem to overcome these emerging challenges. Increasingly 5G and beyond - IoT would be all pervasive moving

IoMT (Internet of Military Things) for strategic applications and IoBT (Internet of Battle Things) for the TBA (Tactical battle Area). Surveillance and Target Acquisition would be outsourced to Space providing better resolution to identify the target and engage with missiles with better accuracy. The Indian Armed Forces, despite the existence of Indian Defence Industry, have been heavily dependent on import of military hardware. It is time that Indian Defence forces lead the Defence Industry to produce high tech warfare equipment ahead of Industry 4.0. This 'lead' must be pushed at least by half a notch creating new 'Military 4.5 standards'. This would need strong R&D, investment in Artificial Intelligence (AI) and cutting-edge technologies.

5G Military Technology Ecosystem Development. This **must** go hand in hand as the civilian roll out is being planned. Immense potential that this technology can offer to the military can only be understated — "5G is not only a leap in communication technology, but also an integration of artificial intelligence, cloud computing, internet of things and other emerging technologies to promote intelligence operations, high-speed sharing of massive battlefield resources, and accelerate the release of its war potential". In a standalone pure communication aspect or with its fusion with other contemporary technologies, there are a plethora of places where 5G holds promising results. However, there are differences when we want to list out the 'military use cases' of 5G. This is due to the differences in requirement and deployment.[1]

Neo-Nanotechnology. This has become an imperative to technological growth and revolution. Light, small, and fast, nanotechnology and miniaturized components offer the military some obvious benefits in terms of portability, protection and connection. But it needs to go further. We need the Military version – neo-nanotech – that's even smaller, refined for reliable performance, and rugged and hardened enough to withstand the rigorous demands of field operations.

---

1 Lt Col Vivek Gopal, "Militarisation of 5G: A Necessity for the Forces", Centre for Land Warfare Studies, Issue Brief No. 291, May 2021, https://www.claws. in/static/IB-291_-Militarisation-of-5G.pdf.

True Network-Centric Operations. These are the soul of modern, Hi-Tech Wars. When target acquisition and robotics are brought together, we will have nearly achieved the Industrial Revolution for Military 4.5. Call it C5ISR-STAR2 (Command, Control, Communications, Computers, Cyber, Intelligence and Information - Surveillance, Target Acquisition, Reconnaissance and Robotics). It's a substantial name for a substantial capability: a networked battlefield where decentralised, robotic-initiated decision making would be the norm. The Command, Control and Surveillance would largely be linked through a combination of space and terrestrial communication networks. These assets communication networks would need protection; how that is achieved is another race. Imagine, for example, that humans pre-program a satellite to identify targets in a certain area. AI can enable them to set the parameters by which the target would be eliminated autonomously - the system would designate the weapon for doing so and take action if the criteria fits. In another situation, humans might serve as the final confirmation before the autonomous system locks-on to a target for action. Another step forward would be to designate pre-sanctioned targets, to be engaged in their appearance.

The Internet of Military Things (IoMT). This would be moving, controlling and activating military resources autonomously for war. Network-centric operations won't happen without the fusion of smaller, smarter sensors, network connectivity, signal intelligence devices, aircraft and UAVs, etc. A secure, private network is the core layer of communicating this data. That will require scalable satellite and terrestrial connectivity for narrowband applications plus fiber and microwave links to support broadband applications. These would ultimately connect millions of devices and sensors operating ubiquitously and support data transfer. AI would play a critical role, enabling the IoMT to transition from mostly telemetry and sensing to complete autonomous action guided by rules defined by individual countries. The IoBT (Internet of battle Things) would control the weapon platforms in the Tactical Battle Area based on precise intelligence and decision control.

Computer networks. These are efficient, desirable tools as they can move massive machine data simultaneously to multiple subscribers. This can also turn disastrous if disruption is caused through technology limitations, an incident driven by adversarial action, or a simple human error. Military has this challenge - it needs its machines and networks secured and protected against these possibilities. High assurances and strong protection tools will need to be delivered by the industry. Call it military-grade secrecy; security protocols would need to be well defined. Secure Chips, Quantum Technology and IP concealment (i.e., no IP Address) would essentially form this baseline.

PME (Power, Materials, and Electronics). PME capabilities are essential for development of any future technology. None of the above will be possible if the industry cannot pin down the fundamental, base-layer PME. Military superiority will come from innovations that can deliver lighter, more sustainable power, perhaps delivered through nuclear, renewables or rechargeable through motion. It will come from lighter, stronger, self-healing materials designed to maximize survivability for the war fighting and bear up under temperatures that span the extremes of heat and cold. It will come from next-generation electronics that are tiny, light, and programmable. It will come from developing the technological mechanisms that make it possible for humans and machines to partner in powerful new ways. PME would expand the possibilities for a single fighting machine to perform operations in all three spheres – air, ground and water – with almost equal efficiency and sustainability.

The groundwork has clearly been laid. We have data, advanced computing, new materials and engineering methods that are translating into the fastest evolution of physical systems in human history.

Human Augmentation. This has already become necessary as mankind continues to build and control smarter systems. More so, as systems become more networked and the machines get faster and even smarter, the sheer speed and connectivity will challenge the human beings they are meant to serve, who will need to keep up. So fast, so capable, these systems will easily outstrip their operators unless some augmentation technology pairs with the person to prevent fatigue, circumvent relatively slower thinking, and fuel a better decision-making cycle. This intelligent augmentation is crucial to controllable autonomous applications. For context, consider the modern-day flight deck, which relies on human input to set up a flight plan. But the execution of that flight is now undertaken by the onboard flight computer, a machine. Why? Humans are now the weakest link in the chain: vulnerable to lapses in attention, fatigue, even informational, psychological, biological and chemical warfare. Autonomous systems are much more impervious to such influences.

Part V: Emerging Warfare Concepts for New Age Technologies

The future of warfare would be dictated by the whole of 'Nation' seen as one warfighting entity and not to be fought by a military or soldiers on the frontline. As is evident, the definition of borders and frontlines would change, the targets would be less visible as such attacks by the adversary would be on the vital infrastructure that makes the nation strong. The centres of gravity would shift from borders to breaking the core strength of the adversary in the hinterland with the combination of means. Technology would make it possible to make things convenient for human existence, unfortunately, it is the same technology that would become responsible for human destruction. In the absence of regulators and Rule of Law for the new era of technology, there would be less recourse to justice. The attacks ranging from Corona to stand-off drone attacks on unsuspecting humanity or an individual makes it impossible to respond in equal measure, intensity and to the perpetrator. This is the complexity of a Hybrid war, where technology would make it possible to hit an adversary while hiding its own identity; surviving through deniability or lack of detection. There would be new ways of fighting battles, with each nation devising their doctrines and strategies. Some of the new concepts which merit attention are discussed in subsequent paragraphs.

Precision Battles. These would make battles more lethal at the point of punishment, decisive yet highly controllable and economic. One of the major issues concerning warfare is that it brings untold misery, avoidable damages and drains the nation of its resources. The purpose of the war is not always to bring misery to humanity, but to defend national interests. In doing so, use of military power is always the last resort. Technology would ensure that the Militaries of the world do not attack speculatively or take decisions based on hazy inputs. To ensure that the Army fights economically, without collateral damage, and applies just military power, it is necessary for the nations to fight precise battles so that the desired end state is achieved earlier and without adding to the burden on humanity. Target acquisition must be done with calibration.

Digital Wars. These would be configured around C5I2-STAR2. Command, Control, Communication, Computers and Cyber (C-5) would ensure all platforms are connected to the Nerve Centre that would act as Communication, Data and a network hub. Information and Intelligence (I-2) would empower decision making and Surveillance, Target Acquisition, Reconnaissance and Robotics (STAR-2) would ensure that the decisions are implemented, modified and delivered with complete impact and transparency. The system of systems approach would be needed to build security and redundancy. Artificial Intelligence and Robotics in warfare would make a paradigm shift in use of technology in warfare. The sensors and seekers would be more efficient and more versatile, giving a rise to a billion-dollar industry where applications would be dual use IOT or IOA (Internet of Anything).

Remote Controlled Warfare. This would be an extension of 'Systems of Systems' Network. The digital arena and the industry 4.0 would make it possible for creating a network with C-5 (command, Control, Communications, Computers and cyber) and connect the machines with the surveillance means enmeshing ground and aerial platforms including drones and Satellites, making ISR a real time possibility. The Sky and Space would provide a strategic vantage point for a decision maker at operational and strategic levels. There would be enough data and information available to decide, cutting short the OODA cycle. It makes it possible for the higher leadership not only to decide but also control operations of strategic importance. With the advent of Artificial Intelligence and Sensors it would now be possible to robotise the battlefield. This would be a game changer as this would be making Remote Warfare possible. The battles can be fought on pre-programmed 'targeting on appearance.'

Network Redundancies. These would be like contingency positions and contingency planning. A military which cannot bring in flexibility of changing network domains at will, re-configure and create flexibility and adaptability would suffer heavily at the hands of adversaries frequently interfering in systems or destroying them, bringing the digital battlefield to a grinding halt. Heavy network security and dynamic reconfiguration would be necessary, without creating any change in the warfighting plans. 'System of Systems' would replace the Net Work Centricity that would factor adequate redundancies.

Low-Cost Expendable Military Inventory. This would be mandatory for the industry to cut costs of warfighting. The rapid change in concepts of warfighting and ever evolving technology makes it important that the war material becomes affordable as longer shelf lives will make some parts of inventory redundant due to shift in concepts. Today, large conventional war machines are not usable due to the deterrence of Weapons of Mass Destruction (WMD). Similarly, Hybrid Wars have made the deterrence value of WMD less significant since the wars could not be completely prevented.

Subterranean Operations. Such operations would be the norm in the era of complete battlefield transparency. This would also be the only way to achieve passive defence, even in depth areas. Tunnelling, borewell tubes and shelters that are not visible from the sky and ground would be a necessity. The logistic nodes, command and control centres and weapon platforms would need to be located underground and underwater. This would need a huge amount of power to run breathing systems with filters, lights and generators. Nuclear power plants may be used for energy. The national Command and Control centres may be located in remote areas and built deep underground, without any signs over ground. Even new multi-storied buildings could be based on 'Well designs' having *minus floors* concept underground. Under-sea Operations would be an extension of the Subterranean warfare. While some work has been done in the sub-surface technologies, the use of robotics would enable better creation and maintenance of underground or subsurface military infrastructure to be occupied by a soldier during war time. Under-sea warfare would be a new challenge to coastal Defence and surface assets.

Reverse Front. This would mean that attacker would turn defences by suddenly appearing in the rear. The third dimensional – vertical envelopment has been the age-old concept, however, with autonomous multi domain fighting machines it would be possible to penetrate through various means and attack more intensely in the rear areas with a combination of rockets, robot-soldiers, special forces and tunnelled approaches. The traditional concept of trench warfare would now be modified to make it possible to penetrate adversary's strongly held ground positions through tunnels. It would be possible for the adversary to be located underneath your positions and even in the rear. Detection of deep underground tunnels through deep penetration radars would be a necessity. High penetration shock waves may have to be used to neutralise underground facilities.

Fighting through Alliances and Collaborative Technologies. They would bring a paradigm shift in war fighting. Data and technology compatibility and long-range vectors would make military alliances work differently. Space, Cyber and Missile Warfare would be elements to pools since they are global commons and know no boundaries. If the agreements are in place and technological compatibility is assured then military blocs could fight in Country groups and /or alliances. There would not be any need to physically fly or sail to another country. In-situ location of resources can be brought to combat against an adversary in a collaborative manner with the click of a button.

Recommendations

The following recommendations are made:

> Need based, Advanced R&D and empowerment of Defence Industrial Complex is the need of the hour.

> Future warfare shall need ICT infrastructure, as a baseline, necessary to power digital battlefield systems. Digital platforms and networks for Tech Based Warfare

need *'bandwidth capacities'* diligently worked out for TBA, War-Zone and Strategic networks. ICT infrastructure roll out plans must cater for standard peacetime (dual use) and surge (Wartime) capabilities. The network should be able to support running of secure and efficient systems based on hybrid platforms integrating complex Radio, line, satellite and EM based networks.

➢ Development of ICT is a long-term sustainable process, comparable to a 15 years submarine development programme. Such infrastructure would need long term, assured and priority budgetary allocation.

➢ We must work our bandwidth requirements for the War Zone, TBA down to consumption for individual units including SF teams Nominate bandwidth per combat team, SF teams. There would be terabytes worth of bandwidth requirement per Sq Km of in the War Zone.

➢ Border Guarding forces must be powered with technology. We need to build smart - digital frontiers for land borders and coastline and integrate it with the overall ISR network.

➢ The Nation in general and Indian Armed Forces in particular need to adopt and infuse AI in warfare. The MoD, Govt of India, through the task force recommendations has made an AI road map, however the Industry and the Armed Forces must collaborate to engineer platforms based on integrated 'Military Use Cases'. The Indian Armed Forces should work on data that would enable writing algorithms.

➢ Robotic Labs need to be set up in the country where digital technology can be incubated for introducing Swarm systems for drones, tanks, robot soldiers. The Government of India aims to achieve a target of approx. INR 30,000 crore by 2025 by exporting defence services and technologies such as Artificial Intelligence and Cyberspace thus making India a world leader in the defence sector.[1] Nanotechnology is essential for ensuring complex machines to be built compact, light and manoeuvrable.

> UAVs have been identified as the weakest link in the Indian capability in modern warfighting. Indigenous UAV platforms are the most essential investment Indian Defence R&D and manufacturing capability needs to address.

> Sourcing of identified rare earth materials like Cobalt, silicon, germanium, aluminium, carbon fibre etc are important to produce indigenous military grade hardware without depending on imports. We need to also prioritise and Invest in the PME (Power, Materials and Electronics) domain to build indigenous systems.

> Cyber Defence and Deterrence must be achieved by ensuring indigenous data centres and securing digital infrastructure. Quantum Technology is essential to create secure and speedy communication and efficient digital applications. Currently 256 bit key that most of the legacy encryptions use need an immediate upgrade. We must ensure that all communication systems including hybrid combat radios are interference free and secure for running IoBT platforms.

> We must set up a minimum scale of Manufacturing Chips and semiconductors for defence applications. Necessary budgetary allocations must be made; industry models based on the Private sector / PPP need to be created. Till the time we do not establish our own semiconductor manufacturing facilities we must establish Test labs for testing imported systems for malware and viruses, to clean up supply chain infections.

> Currently, the world is engaged in 5G/6G adoption. Our industry is still a nascent stage to be able to provide indigenous 5G infrastructure both for terrestrial and Non-Terrestrial IOT applications. Our regulations have to

---

1   Col Sumit Rana, Sydos Paper, Vol. 22, No. 13 (July 2018).

be a soft touch to allow the industry to field 5G systems.

➢ We must invest in warning systems for identification of Radiological, Chemical and Biological attacks. Antidotes must be manufactured and kept ready to mitigate damages that are likely to be caused by CBRN attacks as the Geneva conventions have proved to be inadequate to prevent such attacks. Labs for virology and bio defence must be given due priority. Similarly, we need to invest in weather and nature sciences for military R&D and Defence.

➢ Threat from Hypersonic aerial attack vehicles is palpable. We need to ensure our BMD and AD systems are capable of giving us autonomous shields from such attacks. In the same direction we need our missile programmes to include development of Hypersonic missiles. Similar technological capability should exist through defence shields for EMP and thermonuclear.

➢ We need to cater for digital infrastructure for Integrated, seamless and ubiquitous connectivity for theaterised operations. The AI adoption in the Military leads us to create separate algorithms for IoMT (Internet of Military Things) and IoBT (Internet of Battle Things).

➢ We need to invest in 5th and later 6th generation advanced jet fighters, as also invest in stealth technology.

➢ Space and satellite technology must give us ubiquitous coverage for military grade high resolutions geo-spatial pictures. The IRNSS must have global reach, accuracy and capacity for using it for precision targeting over longer ranges.

➢ In the era of enhanced battle field transparency and longer reach of precision weapons we need to ensure we invest in passive defence in a major way. Subterranean war strategies and surface survival and electronic and physical camouflage from the enemy and weather would be essential.

➢ While Indian Armed Forces must lead the industry by half a notch to move ahead of industry 4.0 standards and adopt Military 4.5 standards. Similarly, industry must produce military hardware for global exports and not for domestic consumption alone.

Conclusion

Military is increasingly becoming technology reliant and therefore industry dependent. Hybrid warfare, the current flavour of warfighting, is fast transforming into a technology-based, non-contact, ambiguous and transitory model. Throughout industrial revolutions historically, industry has been just a level ahead of the military. Today we are deep into Industrial Revolution 4.0, marked by data and machine learning. The current security dynamics dictate that the Military must do that, albeit with caution, to finally pull a half-level ahead of industry. Armed Forces must set the tone for technology-based warfare and create the roadmap so it can reach "Military 4.5" as quickly as possible and guide the industry rather than be dictated by it.

This is a call for the military fraternity and their counterparts in the industry. If a country is inferior in technology, by inference, it would be inferior in national security. Facing an adversary with better technology, you are that much weaker. If you are vulnerable, you are also exploitable by nations that are high on innovation and R&D. That advantage extends well beyond military might. It extends to the negotiating tables, to diplomatic efforts and to trade and financial markets. Overall, security is driven out of accelerating technological prowess. Today China is in a dominant position as it projects and flexes its muscles, leveraging technology and military power in tandem.

Moving the military to 4.5 will represent a major hurdling of significant obstacles including our cultural aversion to swift change. Right now, we have yet to fully subsume the elements of Industrial Revolution 4.0; we are frankly closer to 3.5. The Armed Forces are best to determine what is needed and put forth to the industry. We need industry to deliver today on the most promising technologies of tomorrow.

Author

Lt Gen PJS Pannu, PVSM, AVSM, VSM (Retd) is the former Deputy Chief of HQ IDS and former Corps Commander of 14 Corps. The officer has the distinction of having initiated the raising of the Defence Space Agency, Defence Cyber Agency and Special Operations Division. He was also the Chairman of the National War Memorial Project. He is the Distinguished Fellow of the USI.